Smiling Within

Swamini Krishnamrita Prana

Smiling Within
by Swamini Krishnamrita Prana

Published by:
Mata Amritanandamayi Center
P.O. Box 613
San Ramon, CA 94583-0613 USA
Tel: (510) 537-9417
Website: www.amma.org

Typesetting and layout by Amrita DTP, Amritapuri

First edition: April 2015

Copyright © 2015 by Mata Amritanandamayi Center,
San Ramon, California

Contents

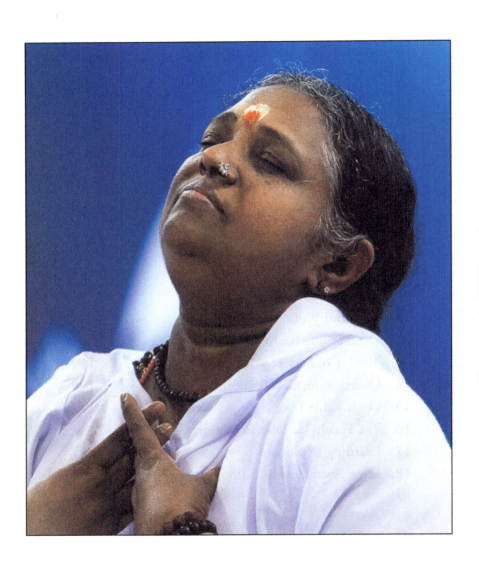

Love was born and came to Earth
In glory and beauty – a very special birth
She walked amongst us in simplicity
Disguised as a human being, just like you or me

She showered us with every kind of grace
Shedding Her tears for all the human race
She looked upon us with Her beautiful, smiling face
Pulling us gently into Her embrace

She placed us so tenderly upon Her breast
Wiping our tears and giving us rest
Holding us close and kissing our face
Saying, "Rest in My lap where it's warm and safe"

She shed Her own tears to wash away our stain
She suffered and laboured to remove our pain
She healed and She taught and She purified
She prayed and She sang and She laughed and She cried

She walked among us and crossed the sea
She travelled the earth calling you and me
She made Herself beautiful and put on a crown
She opened Herself up, and laid Her heart down

Love came to us so that we might See
She came in compassion to set us free
Compassion and Love turned to sacrifice
As She gave to us Her very own life

She gave and She gave, and She gave night and day
She gave and She gave, until She gave
Herself away...

Chapter 1

Choosing Happiness

One day, a young lion asked his mother, "Mama, where does happiness live?" His mother replied, "It's on your tail, son." So the young lion tirelessly chased his tail all day long, hoping to catch a bit of happiness. But after a whole day of trying, he was no closer to happiness than when he had started. When he told his mother about this, she smiled and said, "Son, you don't need to chase happiness. As long as you keep going and moving forward on the right path, happiness will always be with you."

Amma often says, "Happiness is a decision, just like any other decision," but how exactly do we choose happiness?

Many people live stress-filled lives, crazily chasing after inane objects and desires, while losing the most precious of all things: peace in the present moment. We run in circles all day long looking for the next thrill, the next distraction, but we never seem to find the ultimate fulfillment we are always hoping for.

Randy Pausch, a professor of computer science and father of three children, was forty-seven years old when he died from pancreatic cancer. He gave his final lecture to a packed audience a few months before he died, inspiring people all around the world to think of death in a different way.

He knew that he only had about six months left to live, but he lectured with love and enthusiasm. He even showed the audience how fit he was by dropping down to the floor and performing a series of push-ups. He wanted everyone to know that he was full of life even as he was in the process of dying.

He confessed to the audience that although he knew he was dying, he was having a tremendous amount of fun, and he was going to keep on having fun every precious day that he had left. He shared how he lived his life with all of his hopes, beliefs and dreams. Through his example he taught people how to live each day fully, as if it was their last, and how to die with gratitude, awe and surrender.

Pausch inspired millions of people all around the world to contemplate more deeply on the joy of life and the possibility of gracefully surrendering to death. What if we knew we were going to die in a few months? What would we do with our time? Would we be able to leave the world with a smiling memory of us, like he was able to?

Even though we are given so much, instead of living with awe and gratitude, we often find that we feel empty and disillusioned. This is because desire and discontentment go hand-in-hand.

We might think that the unfettered freedom to do whatever we want will fulfill us, but this is not true. As Amma so often reminds us, "Children, sorrow occurs only when there is desire."

Amma tells us, "Even though the outside world is air-conditioned, the mind is not. Spirituality teaches us how to air-condition the mind. Amma strongly feels that this is what is needed in today's society. The mind is constantly burning with desire and people are crazily running for peace and happiness, but they do not find it. Wherever they go there is only unhappiness, confusion, war and violence."

Peace, on the other hand, comes only when we immerse ourselves in loving and serving others. Practicing good values fills our lives with so much more than the comforts of the world ever can. Loving and serving others with the correct attitude is the path to inner tranquility.

We must also have the correct spiritual understanding, or we will always be disappointed. Doing good deeds is essential, but by itself it is not enough. We should make an effort to try and do something good, while recognising the ever-changing nature of the world and not expecting anything back in return.

Unless we make an effort to sow seeds of good actions and positive values, all sorts of anxieties will consume us. Our mind is untamed and filled with an unending multitude of conflicting thoughts, which will bring us some degree of suffering. We cannot completely avoid it. But do not think that we have to intentionally make ourselves miserable.

Whatever we invest our energy in will surely come back to us. Living selflessly with acceptance and gratitude brings us lasting peace, happiness and a reason for living.

When we were in Bangalore for two days of programs, I went on an afternoon walk around the neighbourhood surrounding the ashram. I came across three small children sitting by the side of the road outside of a ramshackle, lean-to shack they must have lived in. The walls were made of torn blue tarps and smoke was pouring out of the tin roof and windows; their mother must have been cooking dinner.

The family was extremely poor, and it seemed like a very unhealthy environment to raise the children in. But still, they looked so happy. The kids sat on the ground near the road, and shrieked with laughter as they played with a small plastic wind-up toy.

I knew they must have a difficult life filled with constant danger because of living on the roadside, but they so happily seemed to forget where they were and instead, were transported to a wonderful world full of joy and peace. What to say for us who have everything but still remain discontent?

Some people choose to direct their mind in a positive direction and be happy, while others are positively happy to be miserable. The choice is entirely up to us.

There is a story about someone who has known Amma since she was a little girl. As a child she lived for several years in *Amritapuri* (Amma's ashram in India), and even had occasional pillow fights with Amma and the other children in Amma's room.

When she was a teenager and entered high school, this girl became very rebellious. She did everything contrary to Amma's teachings, chased every single desire that came up in her mind and had no regard for any consequences. Her parents could no longer discipline her; she was completely wild.

When the girl and her family were preparing to see Amma again after a long absence, she was struck by a deep remorse. She realised that her uncontrolled behaviour was bringing her no closer to happiness and was making her miserable instead.

When she went to Amma for darshan she was filled with deep shame and guilt. She was very nervous that Amma would know everything she had been doing and would be upset with her.

Instead, Amma grabbed her in a very tight embrace and whispered in her ear, "My darling, Darling, DARLING DAUGHTER!" The girl knew in an instant that Amma was completely aware of everything she had done and despite it all, loved her unconditionally. The girl now lives in Amritapuri and has dedicated her life to *seva* (selfless service).

Amma is full of awareness in every moment; everything She does is accomplished with perfect consciousness. She is an overflowing wellspring of positive qualities and She shares them with us every moment of Her life.

Amma is working on many more dimensions than we can even imagine. In order to connect with Her vibrational energy, all we have to do is lift our mind up a little higher than where it usually dwells and open our heart.

When we get too caught up in the world, we easily lose sight of our true goal in life, which is to cultivate love and compassion. Cultivating awareness helps us to keep our focus on this goal. It is the first step along the spiritual path and will ultimately bring us to the highest states of joy and bliss.

Awareness is one of the most important spiritual values we can develop. It is the foundation of all good attributes and spiritual practices. It is from the root of awareness that every other positive and beneficial quality springs. In fact, the whole aim of spiritual practice is to help us develop awareness.

One afternoon when Amma was staying at the seashore building in Amritapuri, She walked out onto the sandy beach area near the ocean. There were very few people around at the time, but one woman was sitting on the sand reciting her *archana* (Sanskrit prayers), focusing intently on the mantras in the small book she was holding. She was seriously trying to practice awareness and intently concentrate on her prayers.

Amma walked up beside her and peeked a little at her around the book, but this woman was determined not to be distracted by anyone or anything. She ignored Amma completely. It was ironic, that the very one she was praying to with such intensity was physically present right there with her, but she did not even realise it. She totally shut Amma out.

This is so often how it is with us as well. We pray to realise God in the highest form that we can conjure up with our imagination, but we remain totally unaware of the true presence of the Divine that is always with us – everywhere.

If we fill our mind with awareness, dwelling with full consciousness in the present moment, we will be able to connect with Amma no matter where we are. Amma is completely absorbed in the here and now, which is why She can hear and answer our thoughts and prayers.

When we exist in full awareness of the present moment, we attain a sense of peace and equanimity and there is no room for the ego to try and squeeze in saying, "Wait a minute; I need some more space." Sorry – no space for ego when we are full of awareness! The ego cannot exist in the mind at the same time as awareness; it will be completely edged out by the fullness of an aware state.

Cultivating external awareness is essential to maintaining internal awareness. It is the most important quality we can strive for. Amma tells us that, "In the light of awareness you see everything as it really is."

Awareness will lead us to devotion, to faith and finally to the realisation that God alone exists.

The God that we are praying to remains with us in disguise all the time, hiding behind every single person and object that we come across, but it takes a tremendous amount of mindfulness to open our eyes and heart to the simple truth that Divinity and love are absolutely everywhere.

If we can develop awareness, then the happiness we are always searching for will spontaneously bubble up, and we will find ourselves always smiling from within.

Chapter 2

Practical Teachings

"The minute I heard my
First Love Story,
I started looking for you,
Not knowing
How blind that was.
Lovers don't finally
Meet somewhere.
They're in each other
All along."

– Jalaluddin Rumi

Amma has often mentioned that a spiritual seeker should develop *shraddha* (awareness), *bhakti* (devotion) and *vishwasam* (faith), in that particular order.

The first time we hear this, we are often confused, but She has explained that only if we develop awareness can our devotion flourish in a genuine manner and blossom into unshakable, perfect and steadfast faith.

17

Shraddha will give us true devotion, which will lead us to real faith. Each of these qualities leads fluidly to the next. We should follow this order otherwise the devotion we experience will be based on our external feelings. Such faith is like the wind; it will come and go.

Amma uses a vivid example to try and help us understand: if a ball rolls out onto the road while we are driving past, we should be aware that a child will almost certainly come next, running after the ball, and so we must be careful and drive slowly in order to avoid an accident.

Even after hearing Amma describe the process of shraddha, bhakti and vishwasam several times, it was still a little unclear in my mind why we should follow that process. Then one day, it all became perfectly clear.

It was one of those days when I had several slightly unpleasant interactions with some of the ashram residents. But I was extremely grateful in the end as it taught me the importance of needing to develop shraddha first. Every situation leads us to something beneficial, if we can open our mind to realise it.

One evening while we were on a South Indian tour, I was waiting for Amma to return to Her room from the rooftop of a building where She had been serving a *prasad* (blessed) dinner.

I usually do not like to crowd around Amma if I do not have to, as there are always so many people who want to be around Her; but I always make sure to be present if there are stairways in order to help Her up or down the stairs. Everyone wants to crowd around Amma and have Her look at them, but they do not think about Her missing a step or tripping because She is busy focusing on giving them the attention they seek (which has happened several times in the past).

On this night, a female resident positioned herself in the pathway of where Amma was going to come down the stairs. Thinking of Amma's safety, I mentioned to the girl that I might end up bumping into her on the way past while helping Amma to go down the steps (as she was standing in the way). I did not dare to ask her to move as I knew her temperament.

She kept quiet, but just before Amma arrived, she leaned over to me and said, "*She's MY Mother!*" It was in a tone that implied that she would kill me if I dared to stop her from getting a chance to touch Amma on the way past. I was a bit surprised, as people are usually respectful to sannyasins – but not when it comes to getting physically close to Amma.

On reflection, it became so crystal clear to me why Amma always says that we must have shraddha first, before bhakti. I finally understood Her statement more clearly and became extremely happy at this breakthrough of sudden understanding.

Many people fall in love with Amma and become very attached to Her, but they do not care about anyone else. Sometimes new people find it very hard to understand the crazy behaviour around Amma, since people may begin to act like wild animals in an effort to get close to Her.

Amma loves for us to have the natural abandon that the *gopis* (milkmaids of Vrindavan) had in their supreme love for Sri Krishna, but they also had an extremely large degree of innocence in their devotion…innocence that we do not often have in this *Kali Yuga* (age of vice). The gopis would forget everything in pursuit of Sri Krishna.

We need to have shraddha in order to be aware of the correct behaviour and attitude that is needed when we move through different circumstances. Our love has often become so calculating that it is sometimes closer to selfishness than anywhere near the pureness of love we could achieve if we developed shraddha first.

Shraddha, or awareness, has a much broader meaning than we often realise. It can also mean trust, faith, belief and acceptance. Additionally, shraddha describes the way in which we perform our actions. To say that we have shraddha, or awareness, in our actions implies that we are acting carefully with alertness and sincerity.

Shraddha leads us to the understanding that everything in this universe manifests to teach us something good, and everything springs from the same Supreme Consciousness. Ultimately, shraddha will bring us to the realisation that God is absolutely everywhere, but it takes a tremendous amount of concentration to develop this single-pointed focus on God.

It is through developing external awareness that we are led to the internal awareness of the Divine. Therefore, we must purposefully try to develop mindfulness in all of our actions. We have to cultivate our awareness quite practically, in order to know how to act at the proper time and in the proper way.

One year as we were driving towards the entrance of the program hall in Mannheim, Germany, one of the girls was so over-enthusiastic about Amma's arrival that she started wrenching Amma's door open before the car had even stopped. It scared me. I grabbed hold of Amma's arm just in case the devotee unintentionally pulled Her out of the moving vehicle.

Enthusiastic devotion is a good thing, but it should emerge from the proper foundation of discrimination. This girl was about to cause Amma to fall out of the car, in her 'high state of devotion.'

If it is our own true nature, why is it so difficult for us to have fully conscious awareness? I believe that it has become a habit to exist mindlessly because we have spent so little time developing the refined quality of true awareness. It is extremely difficult for us to hold onto a genuine state of awareness for very long because we are in the habit of sleepwalking through the world without full focus.

During a darshan day in Amritapuri, Amma handed one of the devotees a handful of *prasad* (blessed food) to be distributed to everyone. The devotee was so busy with other things that she absentmindedly popped the whole thing into her mouth.

Amma turned towards her and asked, "Where is the prasad?" The woman was mortified and just stared back speechlessly. (She probably could not have responded even if she had wanted to…her mouth was too full). In the end, Amma playfully burst out laughing as She could see how utterly horrified the woman was.

Living without awareness is a very subtle bad habit and we have entirely overlooked the great importance of striving to overcome it. We are used to just 'going with the flow' without deeply engaging in the present moment. Because of this it often seems impossible to summon deep concentration for very long.

We can drain away our whole existence on imaginary adventures, carried away by the wings of our mind – never for an instant dwelling in the present moment where we should be. One of the hardest things in spirituality is to simply remain in the present moment.

A few years ago I was invited to go down to Azhikil, a neighbouring village to the ashram, to light the lamp for the women starting their tailoring classes. I used to always get nervous about doing the *arati* (ritual worship) because I find it difficult to ring the bell with one hand while waving the plate of camphor in the opposite direction with my other hand. Everything shakes – my robes, my hands and knees – everything that is, except the darn bell!

When the auspicious moment for the arati arrived I was supposed to light the oil lamp first and then perform arati, but because of my anxiety I jumped right into the moment and did arati. I was overjoyed that it was over, until someone leaned over and whispered,

"You forgot to light the lamp..." A film crew caught the whole ceremony on tape, of course, which only added to my embarrassment.

I joked about it on the way home saying, "That's how we do it in Australia...because we live 'down-under' everything is opposite..." It still remains one of the (many) most embarrassing moments of my life.

These days I am much more in the present moment and if I have to do arati I try not to think about it. Instead of thinking and planning and worrying, I just dwell in the present. Things always work out much better that way (even though I am still the world's worst bell ringer).

Developing true 'awareness' sounds pretty easy. We think that all we have to do is concentrate a little bit harder, but it really is much more difficult than it seems.

Mindful awareness helps our knowledge to flow in the right direction, where it should be flowing, rather than flitting all around the world in a thousand different directions, taking us off to imaginary worlds and imagined situations where we should not be. If we intentionally strive to cultivate our awareness in practical ways, our knowledge will flow smoothly when we truly need it, at the right times and in the right situations.

We have to persistently catch hold of the mind and remind it that it would be better to develop more awareness of the true Self within. *That* is who we really are, but it is very difficult for us to disconnect from the mental chatter in our mind (which has been going on our whole life) and understand that we are not all of the things that we think we are.

We were in the airport one day when a young boy who was sitting next to Amma started talking about a visit he had made to his auntie's house. She had given him chapattis with ghee, and they were very nice. I leaned over to him and whispered, "Is that all you can think about while you are sitting next to the Divine Mother?"

The child replied, "No, I also think about chapattis with ghee and honey!"

Most of us live semi-blindly, ignoring the true potential of what we can achieve with this human birth. When we are able to open our eyes and see the majesty of God's creation in all its glory, we will know true and lasting happiness.

Chapter 3

Developing Awareness

"Fashion your life
As a garland of beautiful deeds."

– The Buddha

We are all on the spiritual path whether we know it or not, whether we believe in God or not. Our human birth, is presenting us with the opportunity to begin a process of transformation into something higher. Evolution itself *is* leading us on the path of spirituality.

Developing shraddha in the form of mindfulness will take us forward on the spiritual path towards the goal of attaining a peaceful life. Even for those who think they are not at all interested in spirituality, a little more mindfulness will definitely help in whatever they choose to do. Awareness is necessary in every aspect of life, not just spirituality. Even a thief needs absolute awareness if he wishes to make a living!

There was a devotee who lost her pencil case. She was positive that it was Amma who took it and hid it. Another girl told her, "No, Amma only does good things. It was your lack of shraddha that lost your pencil case!"

The first girl replied, "No, I never lose anything. It was definitely Amma who took it. It was like this one time when I walked into a bed. I know it was Amma who picked up the bed and moved it into the middle of the floor, because it definitely wasn't there before. I never walk into anything!" How stubborn the mind is. It is always blaming others (and Amma) for all of our own mistakes.

It takes an enormous amount of mindfulness in order to plan anything around Amma since one is always dealing with a multitude of complicating factors, but Amma is constantly ready to guide and direct us when we have not been thorough enough in our efforts.

A few years back in Penang, Malaysia, we carefully prepared the way for Amma to walk off the stage at the end of the program…or so we thought. When She stood up, after having given darshan to thousands of people, we moved the *peetham* (raised platform) back to make space for Her to leave.

A tremendous crowd of people had been waiting outside to see Amma. They had arrived late and were shut outside because the stadium doors needed to be closed in order to contain the huge crowd already inside.

When Amma heard there were still more desperate people waiting outside for Her darshan, She told to unlock the doors and let them in. She never wants to turn anyone away. It was already afternoon, and Amma had been receiving the crowd (without food or rest) since the previous evening. She sat down directly on the ground where She was, at the edge of the stage, and continued to give darshan throughout the afternoon until each and every person had been embraced.

When I checked the pathway on the side of the stage, which had been prepared for Amma's departure, I found a nail in the floor sticking up from the carpet. I removed it in horror of what else might turn up and we carefully checked the area again. When Amma was finally finished giving darshan, instead of walking back the way we had planned for Her, She walked off the opposite side of the stage and around the back, all in Her bare feet.

No one had even thought to check the other side of the stage for broken glass or rusty nails. This is just

Amma's way; no matter how much we may prepare, She always catches us in any momentary lapses of awareness, when we least expect it.

Amma keeps us on our toes because She knows that compassion grows from the foundation of awareness. Without awareness, genuine understanding and pure love are not possible. When we look at Amma's life, we see that Her awareness of human suffering led directly to the blossoming of Her profound compassion and endless patience.

Every day She hears from so many sick people about their heart problems, kidney problems, diabetes and other serious diseases. People from all different walks of life suffer and are unable to cope for one reason or another. This suffering is often due to a lack of food, money or basic health care.

This is why Amma is meticulously careful in teaching everyone to utilise things properly and not waste anything. She knows that many more people can be helped when we are careful with the resources that have been entrusted to us.

Amma half-jokingly says that She has to give an exam to all of the *brahmacharis* (celibate student disciples) who do the ashram's building work, whether they are constructing hospitals, schools or houses for the poor.

During these construction quizzes, She asks the men, "How many bricks will it take to build this amount of square feet? How many cement sacks will it take to build that amount of area?" Amma knows the answers precisely because over the years She has worked out these details for every single aspect of development.

Initially, everyone ends up failing Her exam, as they have never cared to deeply look into all the intricacies of their work. But Amma's guidance and instructions help them to develop a unique level of awareness in different areas of life that one would not usually imagine could be linked with spirituality.

Amma shows us how *everything* is connected and teaches us that we must have awareness in all of our daily actions. We must learn absolutely everything about whatever topic we are dealing with. Our limited selves may rebel at times, telling us that our given task has nothing to do with spirituality, but even so, we must persevere.

Amma never sees one thing as spiritual and something else as lesser and more worldly. She knows the true nature of everything and sees goodness everywhere. Her only thought is… 'How can I give to those in need?' She is a stream of love dealing with all of life's intricacies and hard edges. She teaches us how to correctly manage everything we come across without overlooking any important little details.

For Amma's Amritavarsham (50th) birthday program, the volunteers in charge of the kitchen supplies wanted to buy four million paper plates to serve food for the four days of celebration, which would have created a mountain of garbage and at 3.5 rupees per plate, would have cost a fortune.

Amma instructed the volunteers to buy steel plates instead. At the end of the program, these plates were distributed to Her ashrams for reuse. This investment helped the environment and also saved a huge amount of money, which was then channelled towards helping the poor.

Amma is always able to point out the best way for us to perform our duties with the greatest amount of care and the least amount of waste. We simply do not have the depth of awareness to think and plan as She does. So many people want to take the expensive, easy way out instead.

Amma tirelessly tries to teach us this quality of awareness. She knows it is awareness that will transform the knowledge inside of us into pure wisdom. The well of spirituality springs from refining, developing and channelling our innermost faculty of awareness.

Many years ago, one of Amma's sisters was given a thick golden bracelet for her young son. One day, while the sister was getting ready to go out to the local town, Amma noticed that the child was wearing the bracelet. She said that if the child wore the bracelet outside he would lose it.

Her sister did not listen and left with her son to catch the bus. Just as they were boarding, she noticed that the bracelet had disappeared from his wrist. She was extremely upset and retraced her steps hoping to find the golden bangle, but it was nowhere to be found.

When she entered the house, she was almost in tears. She had not even conveyed the bad news when Amma said, "Anyway, you lost the bracelet, so why cry about it now?" Her sister then remembered Amma's warning and realised that she should have paid attention to it.

We will be thrown into a myriad of different situations as we make our way through the labyrinth of life, but still, we must hold onto a goal, so we do not lose sight of what we really are here for. In the light of such a goal we will find that the external things, which used to bring us so much joy and sorrow, naturally fall away on their own. Acquiring mindfulness will help us to take many steps forward on the spiritual path and attain a more peaceful life.

There is a small girl who takes her Amma doll around with her everywhere she goes. Through the doll, Amma is teaching her so many different things about life, compassion and how to be with people.

This child was talking with me one day, telling me that her doll was taking a nap inside of her sweater. I inquired as to why Amma was feeling so sleepy (Amma rarely takes naps). The child replied that Amma does not get much sleep…She keeps Her eyes open all the time because She just can't stop the love! These little children, in their innocence, sometimes understand Amma on a much deeper level than many of us.

With awareness and discrimination we can drop from the mind into the heart. If we can do this, then we will find that we have not really 'fallen' from the mind – we have 'risen,' escaping from the clutches of negativity into a much higher and more comfortable state.

Purify the mind, and you will find that wherever you look, you see the Divine shining everywhere, through everything. When God leads you to the edge of the cliff, trust Her and let go. Either She will catch you or She will teach you to fly.

Chapter 4

The Art of Surrender

"I was feeling down about life and love. Then I met a woman named Ammachi and She gave me back my smile. Darkness cannot compete with Her."

— Jim Carey

An intricate weaving of the Cosmic plan interconnects everything in this dimension with other dimensions and lifetimes. This plan is complicated, intriguing and overwhelmingly awesome. It all falls into place precisely and perfectly, but always in ways we would least expect.

Even though we cannot begin to fathom the grand scope of the Cosmic plan, we should try to maintain the awareness that everything is Divine will. Only when we have this awareness can we glimpse the real nature of everything and discern how to correctly move within it. This understanding will bring us peace.

Smiling Within

Once in Coimbatore, on a South India tour, the power kept cutting out, and everyone was extremely worried because there was no electricity in Amma's room. Inside Her room, Amma was happily sitting with an oil lamp to gently light up the darkness. She was not at all concerned about the loss of electricity. She remarked how pleasing the soft glow from the lamp was and how it reminded Her of when She was a child. She accepted what came to Her and cheerfully adjusted.

Everyone else was anxious that Amma would be inconvenienced, but She does not think like that. Amma always makes the most of every situation. We must strive to accept everything in life with a positive attitude. Whatever comes, there are no mistakes. We just have to do our best in all situations, as we can never fully understand the intricacies of the Cosmic plan.

Amma turns everything we do into spiritual practice. There are so many people who want to travel with Her. Planning for tours with such big groups takes tremendous discrimination, effort and awareness. It is challenging to foresee the subtle problems that might be lurking somewhere unnoticed, but Amma is the perfect guide.

In July of 2011 we were in Tokyo for a program. It was just a few months after the largest earthquake to ever hit Japan, which was soon followed by an intense tsunami. These twin natural disasters caused unimaginable destruction. Several nuclear reactors were damaged and leaking toxic radiation. Thousands died and intense fear swept across Japan and rippled around the world.

Hundreds of thousands of people were evacuated and communities across the world were worried about the looming threat of radiation poisoning. Amma had the exact opposite reaction; She wanted to visit the affected areas in order to comfort the people there. She understood their state of trauma all too well.

Everyone tried to warn Amma that the radiation level in those areas would be dangerously high, but this did not scare Her. She simply banned any children from accompanying Her and said that only those who really wanted to come should travel with Her. Quite naturally, everyone chose to go.

Amma had a few devotees research the quickest possible way to travel to the affected area, because there is not much free time on tours with Amma. She always plans programs for the very next day after travelling (sometimes even the same day). It was essential that we did not waste any time so that

She would not miss any of the previously scheduled programs. Amma is not interested in taking time to rest (contrary to the desire of most of us).

Tokyo was to have several days of programs with less than one day in between to travel to the next city, Osaka, before more programs were held there. Fifty people wanted to travel with Amma, so we found that the fastest and most economical way to travel the long distance was by camper, mini bus and then train.

Amma is always aware of not wasting time or money while travelling around the world. She has seen too many people suffering for the sake of just a few rupees. She teaches us to consciously manage all areas of planning, striving for the simplest, easiest and most straightforward method to save time and resources.

With this meticulous carefulness one can direct what is saved towards service and charity in order to help those who have so much less than we do. This conscientious planning helps us to cultivate the mindset of true awareness.

As we raced towards the site of the tsunami, our awareness was put to the test. We caught a very fast bullet train and had to change trains during the journey. We were warned that we would have very little time to catch the next train.

A Japanese man, one of the organisers, was very lucky to be able to sit near Amma on the first train ride. He had the opportunity to ask Her some questions. I was lucky enough to hear the answers as well.

The man asked Amma about his personal problems and how he should deal with them while living and working in the business world. Amma answered him with these simple, but profound words, "Awareness and surrender are exactly the same. The quality of awareness and the quality of surrender are just two sides of the same coin. You must learn to surrender to everything that happens to you in life, whatever it may be. We think it's so hard to surrender. People think it's going to be really difficult, 'How am I going to be able to surrender?' But if you really try, you will find that it isn't so difficult after all."

This man got to hear such an inspiring little sat-sang on that first train ride. I was thinking how lucky he was to have something so deep to contemplate on, like awareness and surrender.

When it came time for everyone to change to the next train, this man was trying to look out for everyone, as we were a big group travelling together. He held my ticket and Amma's ticket with him. He led the way, and our large group followed closely after him.

When Amma goes anywhere, everyone loves to try and get as close to Her as they can, and unless I need to be with Amma, I do not try to stay right next to Her. I am often happy to be at the back in a group, so at this time I ended up coming way at the end of the line of devotees.

I followed as everyone boarded and ended up at the very rear of the train. I knew I could walk all the way through the different carriages to the front where Amma was, so I started to do so. But the poor fellow who was holding my ticket did not see me and innocently thought, 'Oh, Swamini Amma, she's not so smart, maybe she missed the train!' Concerned I had lost my way, he went back to the platform to look for me.

Then all of a sudden, the train started to take off. I was safely on board, but this man thought it was better to stay behind and wait for me, just in case I had missed the train and was stranded in a strange place. I felt extremely sorry for him, as it was my fault for not coming sooner, but I also thought he should have realised that I was indeed bright enough to get onto the train. I was not about to be marooned in a foreign country!

As the train took off, this poor man was left behind on the platform, but at least he had our extra tickets to hold onto for comfort, and a beautiful satsang on 'awareness' and 'surrender' to contemplate and keep him company. He received a very good chance to practice surrender straight away after receiving his satsang, and luckily he was able to catch the next train very soon after.

Amma knows that many people become extremely frightened when they hear the word 'surrender.' They think it means they will need to empty out their wallets, give away everything they own and become a beggar, but this is not what is meant. Surrender means accepting everything that comes to us with the correct attitude.

Because the word 'surrender' frightens people so much, Amma advises us not to use it with those who are not yet ready to understand the full significance of it. Instead, we should use the word 'awareness,' as they really are one and the same.

Amma may offer us the most profound teachings, but we have to learn how to digest and practice them in our lives, not just store them in the dusty library of spiritual information that we keep in our heads.

Smiling Within

We do not have to sit down and meditate or perform special rituals in order to engage in spiritual
practice. Just looking into the practicalities of life can
be profoundly spiritual. Simply holding awareness
while we move through the world is one of the greatest, most profound practices we can ever perform.

Chapter 5

The Wisdom of the Guru

"A writer arrived at the monastery
to write a book about the Master.
'People say you are a genius. Are You?' He asked.
'You might say so,' said the Master, none too modestly.
'And what makes one a genius?'
'The ability to recognise.'
'Recognise what?'
'The butterfly in a caterpillar; the eagle in an
egg; the saint in a selfish human being.'"

– Anthony de Mello S.J.

Amma says that constantly dwelling in a state of total surrender *is* God-realisation. Yet who amongst us can say we live like that? Amma knows that none of us have full and complete surrender. In fact, as far as I can see, only Amma is truly surrendered. She surrenders to us, and all of our little desires, every single day.

Devotees often beg Amma to let them perform the ceremony of washing Her feet and adorning Her with ornaments in the traditional way. Amma may refuse them several times because She really does not want to be worshipped like this. Still devotees go on insisting and eventually Amma gives in and allows them to, simply out of Her compassion and Her eagerness to satisfy their desires and make them happy.

The foot-washing ceremony is supposed to be a symbol of the devotee's absolute surrender to the Guru and always comes at the end of a very long darshan program. Very few people think about the long hours Amma has already been sitting, without getting up even to stretch Her legs. Then they expect Her to sit even longer so that they can perform a ceremony of 'surrender' at the end of the program.

Of course, it is Amma who ends up surrendering, by reluctantly allowing them to perform the ceremony. I often think of Her as a 'slave of love.' She humbly surrenders to our desires all of the time.

So many of us unwittingly take advantage of Amma's desire to serve. We should endeavour to place Amma in the position of our Master, instead of making Her our slave. But the impulsive longings in us are so strong that we will often insist on getting our own way, trying to fulfill our unending desires for satisfaction.

Still, we *are* plodding along on the road towards true freedom. We want to go there, but most of us are taking the slow tourist route, stopping to see and enjoy all the sights and attractions along the way. Sometimes it can be so much fun to be lost in *maya* (delusion), trying out everything we can to enjoy a taste of the everlasting joy and true fulfillment we are always craving; but in the end, we will find a big gaping hole where all the fun drains out.

Occasionally we get lost for hours, days, or even years, drifting in the fantasy world of living nightmares that arise when we let our mind run out of control. We invent all kinds of crazy scenarios from our untamed thoughts and emotions.

On the U.S. tour, we usually stay overnight in New Jersey the night before the New York program. Several people who were travelling with us one year, including a young boy, drove in a separate car from New Jersey to the program hall. It was quite a long drive and everyone was tired.

The child dozed off to sleep in the car and woke up as they were driving through Chinatown. He woke with a start and panicked. He told the driver, "Oh no! You've gone the wrong way...we were supposed to go to the New York program, but now we've ended up in China!" In his mind the car had gone in the wrong direction, and he was really worried, believing he was half way around the world instead!

The other passengers in the car teased him by agreeing, "Yes, you're right. We took a wrong turn and now we're in China. What are we going to do?"

When they finally arrived at the program (which took a long time, as China is a long drive to New York) the boy ran up to his mother and exclaimed, "They took me to China! We had to travel to China to get here!"

We may laugh at the boy's innocent mistake, but are we really any different? We so often build fantasies in our mind, usually more intense and much less innocent than merely thinking we are in the wrong country. What worlds are we creating?

Every day we are presented with opportunities directly from the Divine, tailor-made to teach us surrender, but unfortunately we do not often recognise them for what they genuinely are – 'messages from the Beloved.' The play of the mind always comes into it, colouring our vision, looking for a way to manipulate every situation for its own benefit.

For example, if we are lucky enough to hear Amma offer some advice to someone nearby, our mind might say, 'Well, Amma wasn't talking to me directly; She was talking to that other person. This advice was meant only for them.' The mind always wants to escape being disciplined and will twist every situation to find the nearest escape route.

It is practically impossible to rid ourselves of the ego, but if we could, we would recognise the face of the Divine shining through each and every experience in our life. Then we too could embody the perfect surrender that so attracts us to Amma.

Amma always accepts the flow of life with all of its little, inconvenient surprises. Like a river, She finds ways to smoothly and graciously flow around whatever difficulties arise because She knows that the rocks and other obstacles are all a part of the Divine river of life.

When I have the chance to move closely with Amma on the Western tours, sometimes I forget Her omniscience and try to teach Her about the world. For example, when I sit next to Amma on the plane, She might do something unusual like take a bread roll, break a piece off, dip it into Her glass of water and then eat it. Or if there is a small sachet of butter or margarine, She may take it, open it, and eat just a little of it with a spoon.

In these cases, I tend to say something like, "Amma, you know how we do it? We take the bread like this, and we spread the butter on it like this, and then we eat it like that. That's how the westerners do it, Amma."

Amma will enthusiastically reply, "Oh, really?" as if I had just passed on some very valuable information. She always listens to me patiently and humbly as I try to teach Her about the world.

One time She took a chocolate and with a small butter knife cut the top off. She carefully scooped out the soft centre and proceeded to spread it onto the bread, just as I had taught Her…sort of.

Once at the airport someone offered Amma a small package. Later when we were seated on the airplane, Amma opened the package. Inside was a bread roll. She broke off a piece and started to eat it. She offered some to me and to another person seated nearby. She told us, "This is tapioca bread."

After tasting it, the other person disagreed, insisting that it was not tapioca bread, but cheese bread. Amma did not relent, "It's tapioca!" It really did taste like Kerala tapioca. But once again the other person disagreed.

Suddenly I remembered the traditional story of Arjuna and Sri Krishna. Sri Krishna and his beloved disciple Arjuna were out walking in the forest. Sri Krishna saw a bird up in a tree and mentioned to Arjuna, "Look Arjuna, there is a beautiful bird up in that tree. I wonder what kind of bird it is. I think it is an owl. What do you think Arjuna?"

Arjuna, without a second glance at the bird, replied, "Yes, my Lord. I think you are right. It is an owl."

Sri Krishna thought for a moment and then corrected himself saying, "It can't be an owl; they only come out at night. It must be a hawk, don't you think so Arjuna?"

Arjuna once again, without even looking at the bird, replied, "Yes. You are right. It's a hawk." Sri Krishna changed his mind a few more times and identified the bird as a different species each time he spoke. Arjuna did not argue with Him; he simply agreed each time.

Finally Sri Krishna asked, "Arjuna, don't you have any opinion of your own? Why do you always agree with me?"

Arjuna answered, "My Lord, I have to agree with you because I know you have the power to change an owl into a hawk or even an eagle into a swan. All is your Divine play."

Reminding the other person of this story, I said, "If Amma says it's tapioca – then it is tapioca bread!"

We can try to fight against Amma, not wanting to surrender, but it is not a good idea. Some people may argue with Her, asserting, "Amma it's like this, not like that..." Amma will patiently listen as they go on and on, unwilling to retreat, until She is the one to finally give in.

Amma uses the example of two trucks facing each other on a one-lane road. If both are trying to go forward, and no one is ready to reverse and give way first, then neither of them will be able to go anywhere. They will both be stuck. One has to surrender, so both can go forward.

If you want to win an argument with Amma, She is entirely ready to lose. She has said on multiple occasions, "I don't mind losing to you." The problem is, if Amma loses, who is the one that really wins? It will not be us.

If we want to fight against the Guru, then ultimately we will be the ones who fail. Surrender to the Guru is the greatest victory; we have nothing at all to lose except our negative tendencies and the garbage we carry around inside of us.

Amma does not have anything to lose. She lives in a world where She can never be perturbed. We are the ones who suffer from the terrible chaos inside of our minds. We should be ready to admit defeat, and with Her grace, loosen the hold of our ego and be free of the chains that bind us. Only then will we be the real winners.

Chapter 6

Everything is Divine

"All the adversity I've had in my life, all my troubles have strengthened me...You may not realize it when it happens, but a kick in the teeth may be the best thing in the world for you."

— *Walt Disney*

Learning to surrender is one of the hardest things we can do in life. It should not be, but in reality, it often is.

True and complete surrender is a very, very deep process that most of us can only hope to achieve one day. Luckily, with Amma we find more inspiration to surrender than we could anywhere else in the world. But if you do not learn now, there is no need to worry. You will simply come back again and again and again until you do!

As our saving grace, Amma has promised to take birth repeatedly to take us to the goal of God-realisation. Undoubtedly, She will keep Her promise. If we can just try to surrender in all the seemingly small, everyday chances that present themselves to us, then at least we are getting some good practice. We can only strive to do our best.

The Indian tours with Amma provide a great chance for people to practice the art of surrender. We may hear, "Get in the vehicle...get out of the vehicle...get in the bus...get out of the bus..." This may happen five or six times all before we have even gone anywhere! By this point people are often thinking, 'What is going on here...?' But sometimes it is good for us to simply obey and trust that someone else really does know what is going on.

When people first come to India, they are usually ready to question everything: "Get in the bus." "Why?" "Get out of the bus." "Why?" Of course no one will give you a logical answer, even though there always is one – so you may as well stop asking. Somewhere hiding, there is a good reason; there really is.

There is a purposeful reason behind everything, even though it may take us a long time to understand why things unfold as they do. Sometimes it is simply the Divine Beloved testing us to see how much faith and surrender we really have.

A devotee once told me about his experience on tour as we travelled through Singapore, Malaysia,

Reunion Island, Mauritius, and Kenya. We lovingly called it the 'Tropical Trauma Tour' because it was so overwhelmingly hot and humid everywhere we went. After this foreign tour, we returned to Cochin where it was just as hot and humid as it had been overseas. It seemed we could not escape the heat anywhere. We were burning on the inside, as well as on the outside.

This devotee wanted to escape from the heat and intensity of the tour by returning to the ashram. Amritapuri seemed like an oasis in the desert. He was exhausted from the constantly high temperatures, the intensity of the programs and the endless travelling. All he wanted to do was return to the ashram, lock himself in his room, relax under a cool fan and peacefully hide away from everyone and everything.

He heard there was a bus leaving to go back to Amritapuri just before the end of the Cochin program. He became excited at the thought of comfortably running away from the rest of the grueling South India tour that lay ahead.

In the early hours of the morning, he took his luggage, went up to the bus and asked the driver, "Amritapuri?" The driver nodded a 'yes,' so the exhausted devotee climbed aboard and quickly fell asleep.

The driver must have misunderstood what the man had said (or else he misunderstood the driver's head nod). The next thing this devotee saw as he groggily woke up from a few hours nap – was the horizon of Palakkad...for the next leg of the tour. He was shocked, disappointed and a little bit angry, but eventually he realised that it was simply the Divine plan and he must surrender to it.

Sometimes when we really want to escape and make efforts to do so, we find that we cannot escape at all. Our destiny follows us wherever we go. We will all have to learn to surrender at some point. Why not start now?

This man realised that there was an important lesson in the situation he found himself in, and he graciously conceded to go with the flow of it. He ended up completing the full one-month tour because he understood that it was for the best.

God will always have the last say, no matter what we may have planned and decided. Somehow, nature, people and everything in life works together to force us to surrender to the Divine will, in one way or another. If not now, then further along our path, the exact situation we tried to avoid will arise again. It will arise over and over until we learn to face our challenges with the right attitude and accept the consequences of our actions.

When everything seems to be going against us and life seems to be forcing us in a direction that we do not like, let us try to understand that we are being boxed into a corner in order to learn an important lesson. If we refuse, the same situation will return back to us many times in many different forms. There is no escape.

A few years back Amma wanted to bring Her mother, Damayanti Amma, to stay nearer to Her in the ashram. She wanted to keep a close eye on her mother's wellbeing in her older age.

One night, when we were walking back from bhajans, Amma turned to me and asked, "Do you have another place to store your workplace things?" (I was using the room directly under Amma's house as a storeroom.)

"No," I replied. I had only one storeroom, which incidentally had been the ashram's first meditation room.

Amma asked again, "You don't have any other place that you can use to keep all of your things, nowhere else at all you can put them?"

I did not understand why Amma was asking me this a second time, and, without thinking, I again answered, "No Amma, I don't."

Amma patiently tried again and asked me the same question once more. I guess She thought that perhaps if She asked a third time She might be lucky and I would be smart enough to understand what She meant (but unfortunately, it was not to be).

Finally, She elaborately explained to me in detail that She was thinking of turning my storeroom into a room for Her mother to stay in. I was a little embarrassed that I had not caught on and it had taken Amma three tries to get me to surrender my storeroom to Her.

Once I understood, I quickly replied, "Of course, of course, Amma. You can have the storeroom. I'll find somewhere else to store things. It will just take me two days to move everything out." Amma did not say anything more after that.

Later on that night, someone came to tell me that my things should be out of the storeroom by 8 a.m. because Amma wanted to use the room for Her mother and they needed to make some alterations to it.

I felt bad that due to my inadvertent lack of surrender I had not really understood the situation. It took Amma asking me three times before I really grasped the situation and offered Her the room.

If we have love for Amma and try to surrender, even if we cannot surrender completely, it is enough.

Simply having the desire to surrender will bring us some benefit all on its own. It will change the thought patterns we have built up in our mind, and ultimately, grace will start to flow to us. I know that this has been the experience in my life.

When we are facing a very demanding situation it can be extremely difficult to surrender. It is not easy, but we must remember that we always receive exactly what we need, and the things that happen to us are always for the best.

Amma understands what we need. She knows how to help us reach the goal; we should not doubt that. But it may not always be so easy for us to remember this truth when the dark clouds of pain and confusion cover the light of our discrimination.

There is a story about Bhishma, who was a great warrior in the epic Mahabharata. He led a remarkably good and noble life. In the end, as he lay dying on the battlefield, Sri Krishna shot a bed of arrows into the ground for him to lie upon as his support.

Staring up at the sky, Bhishma wondered, 'Why should I have to suffer like this? I have always tried to live a virtuous and pure life.' He contemplated back through all of his past births to try and understand what he had done wrong to cause him to suffer so much.

He declared, "Seventy-three births I have looked back upon my different lifetimes, trying to find the reason for this suffering, and I do not see anything there that should cause me such pain." He could not comprehend why he was being forced to go through such an outrageous amount of suffering when he had tried to live with such piety and honour.

Sri Krishna gently replied, "Not in these seventy-three births, but if you look back one more time, to the seventy-fourth birth, you would see that one day in the forest while hunting, you cruelly injured an insect and purposely dissected it. Because of this, a poor creature needlessly endured suffering at your hands. This is the reason why you too must suffer, even though it may be so many births later. You can eradicate your remaining karma (law of cause and effect) only by being pierced by the arrows that you are lying upon."

We cannot understand anything about the intricacies of karma. From our limited viewpoint, our suffering may seem incomprehensible, but we must understand that there are no mistakes in life. Every action that we perform will have a reaction that will spring from it. Everything is happening to us according to the complicated, ever-perfect Cosmic plan.

Whatever is destined to come to us will come, no matter how much of a tantrum we throw, no matter how much we stomp our feet, scream, shout or curse. No matter what, we must accept whatever comes; there is no other choice. Instead of complaining, why not know the peace that is experienced when we surrender and accept everything gracefully?

Chapter 7

The Strength of a Lion

"Pretend to be the person you want to be. One day you'll realise you are no longer pretending."

— Author Unknown

Someone once asked me, "When should I surrender, and when should I be like a lion? Can a lion surrender without becoming a sheep?"

Amma says we are lions, not sheep. Still, when ferocious voices roar all around us, a few gentle, sheep-like voices might seem like a nice change, but Amma says we have to be brave. It truly takes a lion's strength to surrender in all situations. I am sure we can become brave, merciful lions who use our discrimination.

Amma is always telling us, "You are not little lambs. You are lion cubs, and you have unlimited potential inside of you that remains untapped!" She keeps on reminding us of this, but we refuse to completely believe it.

We carry an inexhaustible powerhouse of energy and strength inside of us everywhere we go. This strength is elusive and we often have so much trouble getting in touch with it, but this does not mean that it is not there. Strength is our own true nature. We should contemplate this truth and strive to imbibe it.

No matter what difficult situations arise in life, we should not give up when the going gets tough. Instead, we must keep moving forward. Being born into this life will always present us with unending challenges, and we are here to face them. Spiritual life is not for the weak at heart; we must become brave spiritual warriors.

When I hear Amma remind us of this, I think, 'Oh, no. I am in the wrong profession!' But somehow, with grace, I am managing. Amma always gives us the strength we need if we pray for it.

There are many different ways of becoming strong. Sometimes strength presents itself as a quiet presence, simply sitting and listening. Our still, peaceful presence is usually stronger and more courageous than all of the aggressive voices we hear crying and roaring around us.

We have to learn to truly be ourselves. Do not look around at others and be jealous of them. When we shine as ourselves, we invite others to shine in their own special way too.

A story is told of a King who went into his garden one morning to find everything withered and dying. Standing near the gate, there was an old oak tree; the King asked what the trouble was. The oak told him it was sick of life and determined to die because it was not tall and beautiful like the pine; but the pine was disheartened because it could not bear grapes like the vine. The vine wanted to wither and fade away because it could not stand straight and grow as fine a fruit as the peach tree. Even among the flowering plants, the geranium was upset because it was not tall and fragrant like the lilac, and so on throughout the entire garden.

Coming upon a little daisy, the King was pleasantly surprised to find its bright face lifted up, as cheery as ever. "Well, daisy, amidst all this discouragement I am happy to find at least one brave little flower. You do not seem to be in the least bit disheartened."

The daisy replied, "Even though I am not of much account, I am happy because I knew that if you had wanted an oak, or a pine, or a peach tree, or a lilac, you would have planted one. I knew you wanted a daisy, so I am determined to be the best little daisy that I can be."

We have to learn to be who we genuinely are in our fullest potential. Amma keeps on urging us on to face our destiny, reminding us that it is our self-confidence – confidence in our True Self – which will carry us through. Self-confidence is the filter that removes all fear.

Fear is very difficult to control because it arises involuntarily. Even if we are using our discrimination and telling ourselves, 'There is nothing I shall fear,' still it may come. In such cases, all we can do is to take a deep breath, invoke our self-confidence and keep on moving forward. With practice, we will eventually find that we can overcome any situation.

Even Amma gets a dry mouth sometimes when She is going to give an important speech, though inside She is never afraid of anything at all. On certain occasions, dry mouths simply happen.

A few years back, after the release of the movie 'Darshan,' Amma was invited to Paris for an award ceremony where She was to give a speech. Just before She spoke, Her mouth became a little dry. Sharon Stone, an American actress who was in attendance, became most concerned about Amma's dry mouth. Amma was fine with the situation, but Sharon went to get a bottle of water.

I was not with Amma at the time; I was translating Her talk into English at the back of the room. I think they poured the water into a soda bottle and put a straw in the top of it. All of us who move closely with Amma know that of course She is not going to drink with a straw, but to our surprise, Amma took the bottle and sipped with the straw. Everyone was amused and applauded.

I looked up from my translation and thought, 'Oh, no, what is happening? Amma never stops in the middle of a speech to take a drink!' But this time She did, because it was the right thing to do in that situation. She was offered something to drink, and to everyone's delight, She graciously accepted.

Later on, while editing the video of the speech, the team cut out the straw scene. When they played the video back for Amma, She had one question, "Where's the bit with me drinking? Put it back in." We were absolutely amazed that She would ask for that to be in the video – She was not shy about it at all. She made the most of the unusual situation and laughed along with everyone.

Often we are so fearful because we think others are going to blame or humiliate us, but as Amma so gently reminds us, "We are all beads strung on the same thread."

Fear and embarrassment are simply elements of the ego that involuntarily arise. They are always subtly there, which makes it difficult to completely get rid of them. But we must be brave, march onwards, and face every situation with strength.

Pain is inevitable, but suffering is entirely up to us. In all situations, suffering is a choice. If we do the right thing at the right time, we will find that life's challenges always turn out okay.

Most of us know the importance of surrender, but our lack of patience keeps us from acquiring much of it at all. If we can remember that we have a lot to learn from every situation, and that the path to surrender is a lifelong journey, we will one day reach the goal.

Let us strive to see every little situation that comes to us as a test from the Guru, or the Divine, designed to teach us something important. On occasion Amma has openly admitted, "I am testing you in every situation." If we fully believed that, surrender would be so much easier, and we would never be afraid. We would see everything properly, in a positive light, and awareness would fill our every action.

On the European tour a few years back, two young children enjoyed sitting as 'apprentices' with the staff doctor when people came to see him as patients. They did everything the doctor did and could often be seen holding the stethoscope and checking people's heartbeats.

One devotee turned up for a consultation and as soon as she walked in, one of the children offered her a tablet. She became angry and scolded the boy, "No, you can't do that. You can't just give people tablets like that!" Later she found out that the tablets the boy had offered her were the exact medicine she needed.

Most of us always find something to complain about. We listen to the negative side of our mind far too often; in fact, it is often our most trusted advisor! But if we can learn to surrender, we will be able to see everything as coming from God. This attitude will certainly take us to the goal. (However, as vital as surrender is, it is still not advisable to be taking medical advice from untrained children.)

It does seem strange that surrender should be so difficult for us because it feels so good when we are actually able to practice it. It is like experiencing peace in heaven when we are able to let go and joyfully accept whatever comes our way.

Everything that we experience in life is a message from the Beloved, grace coming to melt all of our negativities away. Still, it takes tremendous awareness to hold onto surrender when times are hard. Accepting whatever comes to us, with the right attitude, will lead us to the threshold of God-realisation.

Chapter 8

Life's Greatest Treasure

*"If you are depressed, you are living in the past.
If you are anxious, you are living in the future. If
you are at peace, you are living in the present."*

— Lao Tzu

It should not be so hard to make the choice to be happy. Then why can't we? All we have to do is accept what comes to us with gratitude and adjust our attitude. If we could genuinely accept the obstacles that arise, instead of expecting the outside world to twist itself to fit our desires, we would easily find the happiness that so often eludes us.

Two award-winning tennis players were talking together one day. One of them shared with the other the most important lesson she had ever learned. Once when she had been complaining about how badly the tennis balls were bouncing back on the court surface, a friend who was also a great champion replied, "Being negative about it will not change the way the balls bounce; champions simply adjust."

To become a champion takes an extraordinary amount of self-effort, perseverance and discipline. When we learn how to make the most of the difficult situations that confront us in life, then we too will become the champions we want to be. But most of us are just not ready to put forth the effort and self-discipline that it takes to control our thoughts, emotions and actions.

In theory, all we have to do is adjust as much as possible to the circumstances that present themselves and choose to be content no matter what...sounds easy, doesn't it?

When someone asked Amma, "Amma, why can't you make *Kali Yuga* (The Age of Vice) into *Satya yuga* (The Golden Age)?"

Amma replied, "It is difficult. It is better for everyone to make their own changes. It is best to put on shoes, rather than trying to carpet the whole world."

Our lives will always be filled with obstacles. It is best to accept this, swallow our ego and decide to be happy anyway. If we remember that whatever we are experiencing in life is a blessing, albeit sometimes in an ugly, horrifying disguise, everything will be so much easier for us.

Amma makes Herself available to help us through our difficulties, sharing pearls of wisdom to help guide us through life's mysteries. She totally wears Her body away by giving darshan almost every day, in order to ensure that everyone who comes to Her is taken care of.

She tries to make sure that everyone gets personal time with Her when they really need it – even when there are thousands of people clamouring for Her attention. Amma endlessly sacrifices Herself in order to take us higher, but can we honestly say that we properly utilise what She is offering?

There is an old lady from Northern India with two deaf children, who came to Amma asking for them to be healed. Amma said She would pray for them and gave her two small bananas as prasad. The woman refused to eat the prasad because she does not like bananas.

There she was asking for her family to be healed, but she refused to accept the blessing that Amma gave her. We ask for so many things, but we do not want to listen; we refuse to humbly accept the instructions that are given to us.

We should try to assimilate Amma's teachings into our lives. Everyone wants to hear Amma talk. Everyone wants to get close to Her and to touch Her, but do we really want to follow Her teachings? If so, we must strive to put them into practice.

Recently during a program in Chennai, we were sitting on the stage when a foul smell from the nearby gent's toilet came wafting through the afternoon air. Some people tried to burn incense to cover up the stench; I wondered to myself if anyone had thought of going to *clean* the toilet, rather than hopelessly trying to cover up the smell.

I realised that the quick fix these devotees chose is actually a very good analogy for how we lead our own lives. We simply slather perfume on top of every-thing instead of cleaning and purifying ourselves on the inside. We bathe and scrub our bodies, put on deodorant and perfume ourselves so nicely, just so no one will discover our real nature. We walk around with so much trash inside of our decaying bodies and minds, mistakenly thinking that we have fooled everyone, including God.

Amma is offering us everything. She gives us all of the knowledge, the grace, the bliss and the love that we need. She shows us a practical example of how to live through Her own life's actions, but we have to be able to absorb these gifts properly in order to gain the benefit from them.

We have to take the steps to act on the lessons we are given. We cannot merely keep sticking information into our heads; we have to also put it into practice.

Reverend Crystal Boyd wrote a beautiful piece when she was going through an extremely difficult time in her life. She sent her words of inspiration to her friends in an email. It encouraged them so much that they forwarded it on to others, and eventually it travelled around the world, touching millions of lives as it journeyed on and on.

She wrote:

> "Your life will always be filled with challenges. It's best to admit this to yourself and decide to be happy anyway. One of my favorite quotes comes from Alfred D. Souza. He said, 'For a long time it had seemed to me that life was about to begin – real life. But there was always some obstacle in the way, something to be gotten through first, some unfinished business, time still to be served, or a debt to be paid. Then life would begin. At last it dawned on me that these obstacles were my life.'

> This perspective has helped me to see that there is no way to happiness. Happiness is

the way. So, treasure every moment that you have and treasure it more because you shared it with someone special, special enough to spend your time with...and remember that time waits for no one.

So, stop waiting until you finish school, until you go back to school, until you lose ten pounds, until you gain ten pounds, until you have kids, until your kids leave the house, until you start work, until you retire, until you get married, until you get divorced, until Friday night, until Sunday morning, until you get a new car or home, until your car or home is paid off, until spring, until summer, until fall, until winter, until you're off welfare, until the first or fifteenth, until your song comes on, until you've had a drink, until you've sobered up, until you die, until you're born again to decide that there is no better time than right now to be happy.

Happiness is a journey, not a destination."

Whenever someone brings Amma a plant or vegetable that they have grown, She lights up with enthusiasm. Some people might look at the small green gift and cynically think, 'It's just a vegetable,' but Amma knows that joy comes from the way you use your mind. She delights in the feelings of love and respect that inspired someone to make the effort to grow that plant or vegetable. Even if someone simply purchased a plant to give to Her, Amma still acknowledges the love with which that gift was given.

She has enthusiasm and a positive attitude about everything. Amma sets forth the perfect example of how to receive everything in life. It doesn't matter if it is simply a vegetable. Anything can give us joy if we view it with the right attitude.

We should remember that whatever we are experiencing is God's will, and God is only love. It just takes 'looking through the eyes of love' to see the real nature of everything; every little potato, baby tomato and leaf of spinach is a glorious manifestation of God's love. Amma sees the world this way, and She shows us how to see this way too.

There is a great quote from Melody Beattie to reflect upon, "Gratitude unlocks the fullness of life. It turns what we have into enough, and more. It turns denial into acceptance, chaos to order, and confusion to clarity. It can turn a meal into a feast, a house into a home, a stranger into a friend. Gratitude makes sense of our past, brings peace for today, and creates a vision for tomorrow."

When we travel with Amma, we see people who have tremendous wealth – millions of dollars, powerful positions – but still they are never happy. On the contrary, it seems that the happiest of all are often those with very little material wealth. The deepest wounds of sorrow and emptiness sometimes come to those with the biggest bank accounts. When we see people who are happy with very little, it conveys a most profound example for us.

A widowed lady comes from a distant village to see Amma quite regularly. She has two children she is raising on her own. They have only one cow, but with that one cow's milk they are able to make a small living.

Even though they have scarce resources available to them, still they try to make the journey to visit the ashram every two weeks. They are satisfied and have never complained to Amma about any problem at all in the many years that She has known them. They are always happy.

The contrast between what the poor and the wealthy have can be absolutely mind-boggling. But the true value of life is not measured by money, but by the peace in our mind and the joy in our heart. True happiness comes from the way we use our mind. A peaceful and happy mind is our only real wealth.

To become a spiritual champion, we have to learn to use our mind properly. If we learn to control our thoughts and transform our attitude when times get rough, directing our mind away from negativity and upwards on a higher path towards peace, then we can become real champions, reveling in bliss and freedom. To be able to smile when we are carrying a burden of problems on our shoulders is life's greatest blessing and most precious treasure.

Chapter 9

Carrying our Burdens

The Apostle Paul, deprived of every comfort, wrote these words while in his dungeon, "I have learned, in whatsoever state I am, therewith to be content."

— Philippians 4:11

Everyone is suffering in one way or another. Some people suffer in only small, annoying little ways, while others carry a heavy burden of pain right through their entire lives. Only when we learn to control our thoughts and emotions, and strive to live for a higher ideal, will we reach the goal of life.

Some people are physically handicapped, but Amma says that the mind is our true handicap. If we can just learn to still our thoughts and emotions, we will find complete freedom from our suffering.

Many people unconsciously choose to carry their burdens, as they have not learnt even the simplest methods of controlling their minds. They have no ideals or real purpose in life to strive for. Contrary to what is commonly said, ignorance is not bliss; it is the root of untold suffering.

A great cartoon I saw one day illustrates an important point. In it, there was a group of people walking along a road, dragging heavy wooden crosses on their shoulders.

One person prayed, "Oh God, this cross is too heavy for me to carry. Please cut off a little and make my burden lighter; it is too difficult for me to bear." So God chopped a little off of his cross.

They all trudged on with their crosses. Exhausted, the same man asked again, "Oh God, it's still too heavy for me to bear. Cut a little more off, Lord. Please!" So God cut off a little more, and the man staggered on. A few paces later he cried out, "Oh please God, please make this burden lighter for me!" For the third time, God cut away more of his cross, making it quite short now and easy to carry.

Everyone walked on a bit further until they came to a great crevasse with a valley in between. The crosses were actually meant to help them walk safely across the gap to the other side. Everyone else put their cross over the crevasse and walked across the bridge it created, but the man who had cried out to God to lessen his burden was stuck with a very short cross that did not help him at all. He was left stranded, all alone.

Life will present us with unending challenges. We have to use our discrimination to know when we must accept what life brings to us, attempting to be grateful and happy for what we have, or when we should strive to make a change. One thing we know for sure is that there will never be a time in the future without some kind of challenge.

The Theologian Reinhold Niebuhr expressed so wisely the attitude we should take when the inevitable challenges of life arise. His prayer is repeated in the rooms of Alcoholics Anonymous every day, inspiring millions of people who are trying to leave behind their old way of life and embrace a life dedicated to spirituality and service.

"God grant me the serenity to accept the things I cannot change, the courage to change the things I can, and the wisdom to know the difference."

Sometimes it is inconceivable to us why we have to bear the burdens that we carry in life. Whether it comes in the form of health troubles, psychological suffering, family burdens or financial struggles, everyone has suffering to contend with.

I read an article a few years back on amritapuri.org, the ashram website, that told the story of a man who survived a tragic flood in Northern India. When the floodwaters came, his family sought refuge on their roof; many other panicking villagers climbed up to join them there. With the floodwaters rising and too many people on the roof, the building simply collapsed under all of the weight.

This man's family, his wife and all of their children drowned. They died as he was still holding onto them. All of his neighbours and friends drowned as well. Only his sister survived.

In utter despair, he turned to her and demanded, "What is the point of us living now? We have lost everything. We may as well drink poison and die."

She slapped him, exclaiming, "How dare you speak like that! God has given us life. We just have to go on." It was heartbreaking. It made me cry just to read the article. Yet this is the experience of victims all around the world, who have no choice but to endure dreadful suffering every day. We live in a world filled with so much pain.

After the catastrophe, Amma sent Her representatives to help the people recover. The man featured in the article said that while talking with Amma's volunteers he was able to feel at ease and relax for the first time since losing his family. His sister's strength, and the comfort and loving care given to him by Amma's volunteers, helped him to hold onto his sanity.

Because of them, he was eventually able to recover from his personal tragedy and smile once again.

It can be almost impossible to return from the depths of despair when life has dealt us a cruel blow, but there is a magic salve that heals all wounds: the outpouring of selfless love and kindness from others soothes our pain and helps to restore us.

We must cultivate our peace with God and find the faith to know that our suffering is not a punishment. God is pure love, so there must be another reason for our pain. No matter what, we need to summon the strength to go on, knowing that one day all will become clear and we will understand. Amma constantly reminds us that we have infinite potential inside of us to be able to bear anything; the problem is we have yet to find that place of strength and know how to tap into it.

Nothing is ever given to us that we are not strong enough to face. At the moment challenges strike, it is extremely difficult to keep a level head. Often it is only later, when our mind is clear and filled with discrimination that we realise the purpose of the karma we had to bear.

We have to endeavour to turn our suffering in a positive direction; this will save us from relentless pain. If we can overcome our suffering and learn from it, we will be able to help so many other people who are lost in the depths of their own despair. It is from the seed of sorrow that the greatest wisdom can spring forth.

There is a story about an old man who lost his wife. When his friends and family came to share his grief, he met them with a smile saying, "My wife took care of me for our entire life together. I was afraid that I would die first and leave her alone. Now she is gone and I will be the one to face the loneliness, but I am so thankful for that. It is at least one thing that I can do for her."

It is when we are forced out of our comfort zone, into pain and discomfort that we can truly grow. It is then that we find we can accomplish anything life asks us to. Amma reminds us of this frequently, yet we never completely believe Her. We so rarely put forth our maximum effort and ability.

We should sincerely strive to put Amma's words into practice in our lives. Until we do, life will constantly nudge us into difficult situations in an effort to unlock our hidden spiritual strength.

If we allow ourselves to face what life presents to us with a positive attitude, we can help to destroy the negativities that have taken root inside of us. Remember this simple but difficult truth: *everything* is Divine Will. Whatever comes, no matter how painful, is always for the best. It honestly is.

During World War II, the German army raided many villages and routinely stole all of the pigs from the farmers in order to feed their troops. The people were very upset; pigs were the source of their livelihood. They were terrified, uncertain how they would feed their families without their main food supply. The villagers turned to their fields and started growing more vegetables and grains, hoping their harvest would provide enough food and nourishment to survive the cold European winter.

Ironically, because they were forced to cut out meat and eat a vegetarian diet instead, the incidents of heart disease among the villagers went down drastically and their health became so much better as a result. Sometimes what we think is a misfortune can actually be the best thing for us. Only time and patience will teach us this lesson.

Amma often tells the story of a group of snails slowly making their way towards a forest. When warned that the forest is barren and desolate, the snails replied enthusiastically, "That's not a problem at all, as it will certainly have grown into a fine-looking forest by the time we arrive!"

Like these snails, we should never lose our patience and enthusiasm. Patience and enthusiasm are as rare and precious as pure gold. They are truly valuable qualities to have, if we can cultivate them in today's unhappy world.

Amma focuses on joy and does not dwell in the negative. She knows the past, present and future and fully understands everything we get so caught up being lost, sad, angry or depressed about; however, She tries not to let us fall into the trap of dwelling on the bad things in life. She constantly guides us back to our centre, where we can become more balanced and able to choose the direction towards happiness.

Chapter 10

Cultivating Gratitude

*"If we do not feel grateful for what we already have,
what makes us think we'd be happy with more?"*

— Author unknown

Why dwell on the negative things in life? There is a funny story about a baby mosquito who came back after his very first flight out in the world. His father asked him, "How do you feel, son?" The baby mosquito replied, "It was wonderful, Dad. Everyone was clapping for me!" This is the kind of positive attitude we need to help us get through the rough patches in life.

We should resolve to have an enthusiastic and positive attitude as much as we can. So much depends on the way we use our mind. There is a poem called 'Attitude,' by an unknown author that highlights the type of outlook we should all try to develop.

Smiling Within

There once was a woman who woke up one morning,
looked in the mirror,
and noticed she had only three hairs on her head.
"Well," she said, "I think I'll braid my hair today."
So she did and she had a wonderful day.

The next day she woke up,
looked in the mirror and saw
she had only two hairs on her head.
"Hmm," she said,
"I think I'll part my hair down the middle today."
So she did and she had a grand day.

The next day she woke up,
looked in the mirror and noticed she had only one
hair on her head.
"Well," she said,
"Today I'm going to wear my hair in a pony tail."
So she did and she had a fun, fun day.

The next day she woke up,
looked in the mirror and noticed there wasn't a single
hair on her head.
"YAY!" she exclaimed,
"I don't have to fix my hair today!"

Personally, I can relate to this poem because I also have very little hair. All we can do is try to do the very best that we can in the present moment with what little we may have.

Amma teaches us through Her example how to focus on joy and acceptance instead of sorrow. If we watch Her for even a short time (wherever She may be) we sense a Divine joy flowing through Her, from Her and all around. She has found the inner source and tapped into it, showing us that we too can reach this state; it is absolutely possible.

Those with a refined mind and spiritual understanding can 'feel' the magnificence of a Saint like Amma, while others may not yet have an expansive enough mind to understand Her greatness. The depth of our understanding comes from what has already awakened inside of us.

Sometimes it may seem that life is giving us such a hard time. Some days everything seems to go wrong wherever we go. But we have to wrestle with our demons every day – otherwise they may take us over. Only a courageous person can look inside and choose to do the right thing in demanding situations.

Often times it may seem so much easier to take the quick, dark road where our demons are directing us, rather than choosing the 'less-travelled,' *dharmic* (righteous) route. We know which way leads to our spiritual development, but for some reason, we do not always choose the right path. We must not give in to *adharma* (unrighteousness) so easily; we must become fearless spiritual warriors.

Rather than trying to vanquish the external enemies that haunt us, we have to fight our own inner demons first. People do not realise that it is these inner demons that we need to conquer, as they are much more harmful to us than anything else.

I have found that some of the biggest blessings in my life have come from wrestling with the monsters inside. The things that terrify us can become our very best friends once we learn how to control our mind.

Our darkness can be metamorphosed into light, our weakness turned into strength. All it takes is self-effort, a positive attitude and clear focus to transform the scary waters of the mind into a cool, strong river of grace.

When we have challenges to overcome, let us remember Amma's encouraging advice, "Just make an effort to do the best that you can. Undoubtedly you will find that it wasn't so difficult after all."

If we make every effort and surrender our hard work to the Divine, then when we look more closely at what troubles us, we will surely find that there is a hidden blessing in every curse. When we see the world this way, our difficulties are no longer our tormentors; they become the seeds for our transformation.

Dr. Robert Emmons from the University of California at Davis, and Dr. Michael McCullough from the University of Miami, once conducted a study to test how people's attitudes affected the quality of their lives.

In the study, they divided the participants into three groups and asked them to write in their journals every day. The first group was instructed to write about the details of their daily lives, the second group was asked to rehash their day-to-day problems and irritations, and the third group was asked to write about all of the things they were grateful for each day.

The results were inspiring. At the end of the study, the group that focused on gratitude reported significantly higher levels of happiness and well-being. They had more energy, determination, alertness, attentiveness and enthusiasm.

The benefits of gratitude were not just limited to how the participants felt; they transferred to the outer world as well. The study proved that, unlike those who focused on facts or problems, those who focused on gratitude were much more likely to work towards their goals and actually achieve them.

Emmons and McCullough further found that cultivating gratitude *in any way* led to positive changes in the participants. In addition to gratitude lists, some of the other methods that worked included praying, attending religious services and studying spiritual texts.

Some people do not need scientific studies to practice gratitude. One resilient girl I know told me about a game she used to play whenever she felt angry or depressed. She and a friend would get together and take turns saying one word that represented something they were grateful for.

It would go like this, back and forth, "Amma" the girl would say.

"The Sky," her friend would respond.

"Pizza." "Seva." "Ice-Cream." The game had a simple effect: it removed the negativity from their upset minds and put a delightful spin on life.

As the famous philosopher Eric Hoffer once said, "The hardest arithmetic to master is that which enables us to count our blessings." This is very true, but if we develop the strength of mind to force our thoughts to dwell in gratitude, we will know joy.

The world will always be a mess when we look at it through our limited vision, but one day when our vision becomes pure, we will see and experience glory in and through everything. We will see perfection everywhere. We lack this sight now because we have not yet fine-tuned and refined our vision to notice things in this way.

A man who had been blind came to speak with me after having had an operation that restored his sight. He couldn't believe how wonderful the world was; he was looking forward to discovering the beauty of everything.

So often we look around and think it is such a cruel world, but he saw only the magnificence in everything around him. When we attempt to see the world the way it truly is – as a manifestation of Divine love – then we will finally notice the beauty that is everywhere.

We should not waste our time and energy focusing on all the terrible things in the world. Amma does not want us to dwell on that. It merely dissipates our strength. Instead, She urges us to develop compassion. It is our duty to feel empathy for the suffering and try to do what we can to help those in need, in any way we can.

There are so many inspiring people in this world. There are those who were involved in dangerous or illegal activities and somehow found the strength to turn their lives around. Many of them choose to go back to the same dangerous streets they came from in order to help others overcome lives of violence and crime. Their lives have been chiselled out of tough experiences, yet they inspire so many to change for the better.

We should use the talents and experiences we have gained in our life to reach out and help others (that is why God gave them to us). In this process all of our own sorrows will melt away and be forgotten.

Amma often says if we spend even one second showing kindness to another person, making them happy, that all on its own is a very great thing. This is something each one of us can do. Only this present moment is in our hands – so we should try to do good things now.

People all over the planet are becoming aware that we need to take better care of Mother Nature as well as our sisters and brothers all over the Earth. Surely the positive vibrations of these spiritually minded people will have a positive effect on our ailing world.

If all we do is think about our own needs, disregarding everyone else, then we will only become selfish, insensitive and depressed. We can end up sinking down so low and wasting our entire life wrapped up in self-centredness.

Amma says that there is always someone who is looking up to us, taking us as their role model, even if it is just our younger brother or sister. Perhaps if we do incredibly good things, even in the very smallest of ways, others will follow our example as well. Slowly, step-by-step, we can change the world…

God has created such a magnificent world. The suffering and negativity we see are not God's creation, but our own. We have created suffering with our uncontrolled minds and egos. Amma is showing us another way forward. Unlike us, She sees the Divine wonder in everything, and this gives Her the highest joy that can ever be attained.

Amma dwells entirely in the present moment. That does not mean that She sits back and quietly enjoys the splendour of God's creation. There is no one who has ever worked harder or longer than She does. She gives Her absolute maximum in every situation and takes the absolute minimum for Her own personal needs. No one has ever put more personal energy into serving the poor and needy than Amma.

Chapter 11

Love and Work

*"The best antidote I know for worry is work.
The best cure for weariness is the challenge of helping
someone who is even more tired.
One of the great ironies of life is this:
He or she who serves almost always benefits
more than he or she who is served."*

— Author unknown

Amma teaches us that hard work is the secret ingredient that brings true success and happiness in life. We cannot rely on grace alone; we must also put forth effort. In truth, grace can only come from effort.

There was a woman who came to see Amma for the first time in Los Angeles and then flew to India to come on the North India tour. She is a make-up artist in L.A. and works in Hollywood with all the big stars.

She was talking about her seva on tour, saying,

"I am doing juice stall seva, which is nice, but I feel like I've kind of lucked out, because the shift before us does all the work, so when I come, they always say, 'Just cut some limes and then you can go.' So I always leave early and just go sit on the stage with Amma.

Then one day Amma just kept staring at me, and I felt like she wanted me to get dirty doing some actual seva. So I walked off the stage and ran into a woman who was going to pick up litter; we started to pick up the trash together. It was really humbling.

A lot of people were just staring at me in my whites, picking the garbage up off the street. Sometimes they would snap their fingers at me and point out more trash to pick up off the ground – of course they wouldn't move at all to pick up anything themselves. But then I really started to enjoy the seva. I was thinking, 'I really like this dirty seva! Well heck, I should pull out my apron every day and do this!'

Then the second day, I was really excited to do 'real' seva again. I had figured out what to do, where to put the trash after we had collected it, etc. My hands were all filled with garbage and my clothes were getting dirty, it was really thrilling.

Then some devotees stopped me and asked, 'Can we take your picture?' My picking-up-trash partner said, 'Come on! Let's go!' but I told her, 'Gimme a minute here! I need to take care of the people!' So I fixed up my hair and brushed myself off and posed for them with my pick-up stick. (I thought to myself, 'This could go on Facebook somewhere!')

Then after I had finished my seva, after an hour or so I had a shift with Amma on the stage. Amma turned around to look at all the people sitting by Her. Then she turned to look at me directly and gave me a nod of deep approval."

The only thing a genuine spiritual Master wants is for us to be happy, so they try to inspire us to put forth the effort it takes in order to attain our own peace of mind. Amma is unique and has Her own goal: She wants us to attain bliss, the same bliss She has tasted, and She will do whatever it takes to bring us to that state. Our part is so simple in essence, yet it is very difficult for us to put forth the effort required to achieve this goal.

One day Amma said, "To see My children in the state of *samadhi* (bliss) would be just like..." She gestured as if She was drinking Divine ambrosia. A blissful look beamed on Her face as She said this. It was beautiful to see how it could be for us, if only we would really try.

Amma repeats again and again, "My children's happiness is Mother's food. Amma's happiness is when you find bliss within yourselves."

We have to pay a price to attain the state of highest ecstasy; it takes an awful lot of hard work. We should not be lazy. Amma is urging us to make persistent efforts so that we can find the Supreme joy.

Amma practices the most gracious and effortless effort, naturally and spontaneously in everything She does. During Her 61st birthday celebration, while someone was giving a speech about Amma, he remarked how, "Amma works seven weeks, every day."

At first, I laughed to myself a little thinking that it was just a small slip of the tongue. But after thinking it over, I realised that his words were actually most apt and completely true. Amma *does* do seven weeks worth of work in every single day! No one else in the world accomplishes anywhere near what Amma is able to.

We often hear something and judge it according to our limited mindset, but if we expand our thinking a little more, we will discover there are other hidden levels of existence beyond our wildest imaginings. At the moment, we have no understanding of these at all. When we gain a certain degree of humility it expands our vision and an entirely bigger world of possibilities starts to unravel.

Amma has given us everything we need to live a rich and rewarding life. There is nothing more that we need in order to reach the goal. We have a perfect Master, spiritual books to teach and inspire us available in the library or bookstore, and bhajans for those who want to feel the bliss of devotion. Amma makes it possible to regularly receive the touch of a Perfect Master, and we have nearly endless opportunities to serve others; *everything* is available with Amma.

Those of us who get to be with Amma all the time are so spoilt, we absolutely are. We just have to extend ourselves in some kind of effort and Her grace will come flowing to us like a river.

As Kahlil Gibran, tells us, "Work is love made visible." Love for Amma bestows an incredible wealth of strength on Her devotees who routinely go on working for days and nights in whatever capacity may be needed.

The visible love of Amma's children takes so many different forms: physical work during disaster relief operations, sitting and working in front of the computer for hours on end, organisational planning for Amma's many charity projects and programs or even simply folding and passing Matruvani magazines to get them ready for their posting dates.

Amma says it is better to wear ourselves out doing something good for the world, rather than rusting away. She inspires millions of people to offer service to the world.

When She was growing up, Amma's mother urged young Sudhamani to constantly pray to God to give Her work. Instead, Amma would pray, "Please God, always give me *Your* work." God's grace flows to the one who is always ready to help others.

Amma's mother always worked very hard and influenced Her children to be like this as well. When Amma was young, even if She was completely exhausted, Damayanti Amma told Her that She should never show it. Instead, She should always maintain a positive attitude and be happy to take on even more work. Her mother would never make anyone do anything for her; she was self-reliant and always did things for herself.

Damayanti Amma rose at exactly three a.m. every morning, a practice she continued throughout her whole life. After rising, she did all of the housework and chanted traditional mantras and prayers for three to four hours until the sun rose.

Once the sun was up, she would immediately go outside and prostrate. Her rule was that the courtyard should be completely swept before the sun rose. She believed that one should never show the broom before God. She knew the value of hard work and the wisdom of ancient traditions – and she passed these values on to her children.

As a child, Amma's work ethic often annoyed Her sisters. She never let Her sisters sleep late in the morning, but instead made them get up at four a.m., light the lamp, bathe, and help with some work. They used to be so mad at Her for making them get up so early in the morning. By the time that everyone else in the neighbourhood woke up, Amma's family was already done with all the work in the house and ready to go.

The neighbours praised Amma's family and told their own relatives that they should learn from this example. They would say, "See how they get up and do all their housework?" The old man next door always got up early to take a bath, while his wife and children slept comfortably. He would start trouble with his family by comparing them with Amma's family saying, "Look at the people next door, they are so disciplined!"

In the afternoon, Amma and Her sisters used to go out to cut grass for the cows. Amma never minded to do the cutting but the other sisters did not like digging or washing the grass, as their hands would get dirty, so they would fight over getting the least dirty work to do.

The sisters still vividly remember how quickly Amma did everything; She took care of the cows, cut the grass and did all of the housework so fast that they could never catch up with Her. Besides all the work Amma did, She still paid attention to all of Her family's needs and made time for devotion and meditation as well.

When we give of our time and energy to serve, we realise that we are capable of accomplishing amazing things. So many devotees have found this to be true in their lives. The more we work to serve others, the more grace and joy will flood into our lives.

When a survey was conducted to see if people would quit their jobs if they ever won the lottery, surprisingly nearly everyone replied that they would be happiest continuing to work. Most people enjoy working. Even if they find it difficult at times, they know they must work not just to earn money but also to maintain a certain amount of peace in their lives. The peace we experience when we do service work is unique; it is an especially deep peace that we often cannot quite put into words.

I once heard a very touching story about a heroic woman who made her job into pure service. From the time she was a young girl, she had always wanted to be a teacher. As an adult, she helped countless difficult students to successfully navigate their way through the school system. Then suddenly, she was stricken with Lou Gehrig's disease, which is usually fatal within a mere five years.

When the disease was diagnosed, she wrote an email to her colleagues and all of the families of her students. She let them know that she had one final lesson to teach them: that death is a natural part of life.

She requested to stay at her job, communicating by computer when her voice left her. She never wanted to go home to rest like most people would have wanted to, but instead, started to manage two elementary school libraries. Her colleagues all unanimously named her "Teacher of the Year."

Selfless service is the easiest way to forget who we think we are. It helps us to discover the Divinity inside of ourselves and inside of others as well. It is one of the most beautiful and easiest paths to follow. The key to joy and peace is so simple: just do your best to do something good, no matter how small it may be.

Chapter 12

Overcoming Sorrow

*"Kind words can be short and easy to speak,
but their echoes are truly endless."*

— *Mother Teresa*

Amma offers us the perfect opportunity to earn good karma by providing innumerable different situations to perform selfless service. Working hard for a good cause, with the right understanding, creates a beautiful flow of joy in us. Seva really is one of the easiest, most gratifying spiritual practices there is.

On the rare occasion when Amma is in Her room and has not given people darshan that day, She will refuse to eat. She says we should do at least a little work every day to earn the food that we eat. Then after that, we should do a little more seva to help others in need. Amma makes it quite clear: if we hope to progress, there is no escape from the necessity of hard work.

We have to perform selfless actions or we will become selfish and lazy. Even people with physical disabilities do seva around Amma all the time: greeting newcomers, checking wristbands, security seva... selfless service does not have to be manual labour. Offering prayers for others is also seva because we are not thinking of our own needs.

It is virtually impossible to avoid seva around Amma, especially when we see Her working so hard. We may as well humbly give in, with a surrendered attitude, and determine to work with the best possible attitude that we can muster. It really is for our own good, as our actions and attitudes are going to follow us like a shadow everywhere we go, right into the future.

There is no escape from our past karma; it will have to bear fruit. But if we are ready to pitch in and help whenever the need arises, we will be able to cut through many of the karmic chains that bind us.

We will not always be able to maintain the perfect attitude. After all, it can be difficult to stay cheerful when you are knee-deep in cow manure, shovelling it on a hot day as an ocean of sweat threatens to drown you. But rest assured, a large deposit will be placed in your karmic bank account. When we make our self do something good because we know it is the right thing to do (even if we really do not want to), a torrent of grace will flow to us.

It is often hard to force our self to do what is needed, so we should not waste time thinking about whether we feel like it or not. We need to jump in and resolve to do something good before the mind talks us out of it. We are so lucky when we receive the chance to perform service; seva really is one of the sweetest spiritual practices.

Our mind is always churning. It is the mind's tendency to always want to drag us down. When we undertake the responsibility of seva however, we get the opportunity to pour our energy into something beneficial. This lifts us up and prevents the mind from diverting our energy down and out into negativity.

When you are feeling depressed and try to sit quietly in meditation on your own, then undoubtedly, disturbing thoughts will start to arise. Amma advises that when we are troubled, it is best to keep busy instead.

People who have psychological problems, or any tendency towards depression, should not be left to sit idly with their uncontrolled mind. The mind will spin even more wildly, bent on bringing even more misery. Instead, they should be encouraged to keep busy doing something interesting, no matter what it is.

The goal should be to capture our restless mind and give it something good to focus on, something less destructive than it would choose on its own volition. Seva is so good for us because it lifts us out of our isolated, selfish little world in order to help others.

There is a devotee who came to India to work for Amma, who was sent to Mumbai to do some seva there. A few months later, as he was on the train coming back to visit Amma in Amritapuri, he was feeling a little sad and neglected. 'Perhaps Amma has forgotten me,' he thought to himself. At that exact moment, he received a text message from a friend telling him that Amma had just been talking about him and was praising him.

Amma is always with us, guiding our every thought and action. She reminds us that She is constantly watching over each one of Her children. Amma is the quiet voice inside of us whispering words of wisdom to keep us out of harm's way. She speaks to us in such a subtle, gentle voice that we may not always hear Her – our likes, dislikes and selfishness create an awful lot of chatter in the mind – but we should never doubt Her presence.

As Amma reminds us, "With pure love there is absolutely no distance at all between us."

In Brisbane, Australia, when the program had finished and Amma was walking towards the exit, She noticed a man standing behind the line of people gathered along the path to say goodbye to Her. She asked him if he had received prasad and I asked him if he had received darshan. He said, "No, I am just a volunteer driver." Amma kissed his hand sweetly.

Even if it is just one person amongst the crowd, a single face amidst the sea of people, Amma recognises those She has not embraced. Sometimes at the end of the last program in a city, after She has seen so many thousands of people, when Amma walks through the crowds to leave She will spot someone who has not come to Her. Perhaps they did not come because they could not get a token, or because they felt the crowds were too big, or because they know Amma suffers pain in Her body from giving darshan for such long hours.

Amma knows which of Her children have not received darshan, and She often embraces them on Her way out of the hall. For those who choose not to go for darshan in order to save Her the strain of seeing one more person, Amma always acknowledges their sacrifice in one way or another. She is always conscious of everyone and everything around Her and She showers us with so much grace.

We have lived through many different lifetimes. We have done it all: we have been men; we have been women; we have been married; we have been celibate. We have been given so many gifts in life, over and over again. Now it is time for us to reach out to others and do something to pay it back.

At some point in our evolution we have to strive to rise to the highest place we can reach and joyfully give back some of the countless blessings we have received. If we can do this, the blessings will only keep on multiplying.

A devotee tells a story:

> "We started an Embracing The World seva called 'Amma's Hands.' Amma's physical body can only be in one place at a time, so Amma's devotees are Her hands out in the world. A lot of times devotees have an urge to help and serve, and are so inspired by Amma when they see Her, but then they go back into their regular life and not many people follow through with things. 'Amma's hands' is an attempt to change that.

We go into nursing homes and work with people who are dying. They are all in wheelchairs and they need help with everything. They can't eat by themselves and they are completely alone. They are all very sick, struggling and scared, and they don't have families to comfort them because it is too hard on the families to see them in such a state.

We go into the nursing homes and do healing sessions with them. We also bring them things like prayer shawls and give them massages. One lady paints their nails to make them feel like they are loved and cared for. We read to them and sing with them. We just try to be present. Being present with someone is the biggest gift you can give.

This seva is making a huge difference in their lives. They are starting to smile again – and always ask when we are coming back. When we visit, it gives them hope. They reach out to us, grab our faces and kiss us saying, 'Thank you,' almost crying.

We also give massages to the caretakers, because the environment is so stressful for them as well. My goal is to involve as many of Amma's children as possible. Amma's message is about helping those in need, first and foremost.

My wish is to inspire other people to start this, as much as possible. So far 'Amma's Hands' is in Boston, and we are spreading to Europe as well. We *are* Amma's hands. We need to be out in the world, serving Her. We should strive to be with people the way She would be – with as much love, compassion and dedication as possible, as if we are Amma's own hands serving each one of them."

Often we misjudge what it means to be truly spiritual. People sometimes say, "Oh, I'm not spiritual...I just try to be a good person." Others consider themselves to be deeply spiritual, but everyone else considers them just plain mean. Kindness is a manifestation of spirituality in its truest sense. We should strive to be kind. It really is not so difficult.

The one who is ready to smile a genuine smile at everyone is quickly scaling the heights of spirituality. Those who are ready to help anyone, in any way they might need, know that service to others is true spirituality.

All spiritual practices are designed to unlock our awareness so we can concentrate and dwell in this present moment and, just like Amma, let the love flow wherever we go. Do not think we have to suffer. Selfless service will lead us home to true freedom and bliss.

Chapter 13

The Joy of Service

*"As you help those in need, selfishness will
fall away, and without even noticing you
will find your own fulfillment."*

— Amma

Grace will come when we perform good actions with
a selfless attitude. If we determine to do something
good we will discover the magic formula to tap into
the Guru's grace, even if we may not go anywhere
near the Master's physical form.

A few years ago while we were on tour with Amma
in Palakkad, it was extraordinarily hot. It is usually
hot in Southern India but this particular year, the
heat and humidity were beyond extreme. We were
all unquestionably suffering. I was working in my
room as Amma was giving darshan, doing my best
to survive the heat, when someone came in and said,
"Come along and help us chop vegetables, a change
of seva will be really good for you!"

I thought, 'Uh, thank you. What a great suggestion! That will really make my day, going out there into the scorching hot, mid-day sun to chop vegetables...' But then I caught myself and thought, 'Ok, this might actually be a good idea.' I reminded myself that this suggestion was a message from the Beloved trying to teach me something good.

I usually stay in my room while we are on tour and work on my books or other seva projects I have brought along. Chopping vegetables was a completely different seva than I was used to (although I was a veggie chopper thirty years ago when I first came to the ashram). So, I went outside and down the road a little to a tent-like structure that had been constructed for the vegetable choppers and sat down in the heat to cut vegetables with a few other people.

I was completely shocked by the experience – I had forgotten that cutting vegetables could be so much fun – even if it was cabbage day. You have to cut an awful lot of cabbage to create a meal that feeds everyone. You just go on cutting and cutting...

There were seven huge containers full of cabbage but no matter how many cabbages we cut, the containers always remained half full. I am sure it was Amma playing games with us, manifesting more and more cabbages for us to chop! The funny thing was, despite the heat, and despite the never-ending cabbage, vegetable cutting was such a bliss-filled experience.

Everyone was so happy. It was so joyful to see how everyone managed and how surrendered and jovial they all were while doing their seva. I became blissed out just watching everyone.

There was a young girl, only three years old at the time, who was discovering the joy of selfless service. She was getting the plates of cabbage from everyone and putting them into the big container. She was bubbling over with excitement while doing this because it was such a fun game for her. It was amusing and rewarding to get to watch her discover the beauty of selfless service.

One boy was working on a song he had written for Amma. It was pretty dreadful really, but just hearing him sing his little heart out, practicing his song in the sweltering heat, was somehow charming. He was not shy at all about innocently and enthusiastically performing his composition. I knew Amma would love it.

An older man, who could hardly speak English, was leaving the tour the next day. I thought how great it was of him to sacrifice his time doing seva, cutting vegetables, when he had such precious little time left to spend with Amma. He could not talk to anyone so he was quietly cutting away, even though he could have been watching Amma instead.

Suddenly, the man cut his finger. He went off to get some first aid and put a bandage on it. I felt really sad that he had hurt himself and expected it was the last we would see of him. But he came back to continue chopping even though there was a heavy bandage on his finger to cover the wound. I was so impressed by the sincere attitude of all these people.

A teenage boy who was present said we should have the speaker system on, as there was no music coming through to where we were chopping (and he quietly told us that he would rather hear the swamis sing than this other boy practising). He excused himself, declaring that he was going off to get the speaker box connected. I assumed the boy just wanted a way out, an escape from the never-ending cabbage.

I thought, 'That's the last we're going to see of this kid. What a great excuse to get out of here. Goodbye teenager, we'll never see you again!' Who expects a teenager to be sitting in the heat, cutting cabbage, anyway?

Twenty minutes later, he returned and the music was on. I was shocked once again. Before I knew it, this young boy was happily back to his seva, and he wasn't alone. He had brought both of his parents with him. We are used to seeing many dysfunctional families in the West, but here was a genuinely 'functional' family. They all looked so happy to be together, sitting and working, enjoying chopping the endless buckets of cabbage.

These people all had imbibed the correct attitude of selflessness and surrender and were able to turn a miserably hot day into a day filled with the cool breeze of Guru's grace.

It is rare to find groups of people who perform their duties with so much joy, dedication and surrender, but we can find examples of this everywhere around Amma, especially in the countless charitable projects that are done in Her name.

Many people are happy doing the less glamorous sevas like cleaning toilets or sorting the trash. Although they are physically far away from Amma, they are often far happier than those who spend endless hours sitting close to Her, simply staring at Her.

There are also those people who will only do seva when Amma turns up so that She will see them working – but they are not usually the merriest of people at other times. It is really amazing how many people will turn up to work when Amma comes. They will grab a broom or something that they never would have touched before. It is as if they are thinking, 'Amma's here! Quick, everyone look busy.' But when we come across the people who are happily doing seva far away from Amma without any expectations, it is one of the most beautiful, inspiring sights we can see.

Amma is not limited to Her physical body. She knows our mindset, wherever we may be. When we are doing good things with a selfless attitude, Her grace will surely flow to us no matter where we are in the world. Selfless service truly is the deepest form of devotion and moving meditation.

When we perform noble actions, our lives become blessed, no matter if Amma can physically see them or not. We do not need to be doing seva close to Her in order to experience Her grace. Just as iron filings are drawn to a magnet, it is the Cosmic plan that grace will find us when we do good deeds.

It is selflessness that brings us joy, not seeking things for ourselves. Everyone knows that the greatest joys in life are free: watching a sunset, helping someone in need, seeing a child's face when they smile, receiving a look from Amma, or doing selfless service. These simple things bring authentic joy into our lives.

If we are merely fulfilling our desires, there will always be more desires that come to replace them. Desires are endless. But if we try to dissolve our desires for personal fulfillment in the ocean of seva, we will find more peace of mind than is available anywhere else.

We are so blessed to experience the beautiful environment Amma creates for us everywhere She goes. There are so many people around Her serving others without any expectation of reward. You will never find any other place in the world imbued with such a deep peace, where so many different people are living together, as you will in Amma's presence.

Everything is extremely successful in Amma's organisation because grace and selflessness form the foundation behind the creation and growth of everything connected to it. Amma's Ashram in India is particularly powerful because the birthplace of a Saint holds an extremely potent and purifying energy.

Decades ago, when we were first building the ashram, we never had a single wheelbarrow or piece of machinery, but still we managed to construct the temple and other buildings. The bell used to ring during the day, not to call us for scriptural classes, but to call us for seva.

We moved sand by throwing saucer shaped metal bowls of cement to each other, which we passed down from person to person along a line. We carried rocks and bricks on our heads from one place to another.

Amma was always there, working alongside us, inspiring us and urging us on.

Everyone was so happy doing all of this construction work – even when our hands were rough and burning, and the skin started to peel away with the cement. Occasionally it would even turn into a competition to see who had the most damage to his or her hands. The skin grew back slowly, but our spirits rapidly soared.

My hands are so soft now; it is sad. Very few people were lucky enough in that time to have had the chance to do so much intense manual seva with Amma – those days were precious. But even today Amma occasionally creates opportunities for everyone to serve together like this. Hard work can be so good for us. It is important to keep our body, mind and thoughts in shape by working hard for a good cause.

We are always engaged in action, even if we are just thinking. Our thoughts are constantly running around in circles worrying about one thing or another: what we have to do next, what someone is saying about us, how we are going to earn a living, etc. Always the mind is whirling around manifesting some problem or another.

The great spiritual Masters of India have always taught us that in order to channel the mind into a positive direction we need to make an effort to control it with spiritual practices. If we hold the attitude that all of our energy, every thought, word, and action is an offering to the Divine, then our mind will begin to be cleansed and purified.

We should take the energy and blessings we have been given in our life and transform them into gifts to be shared with humanity.

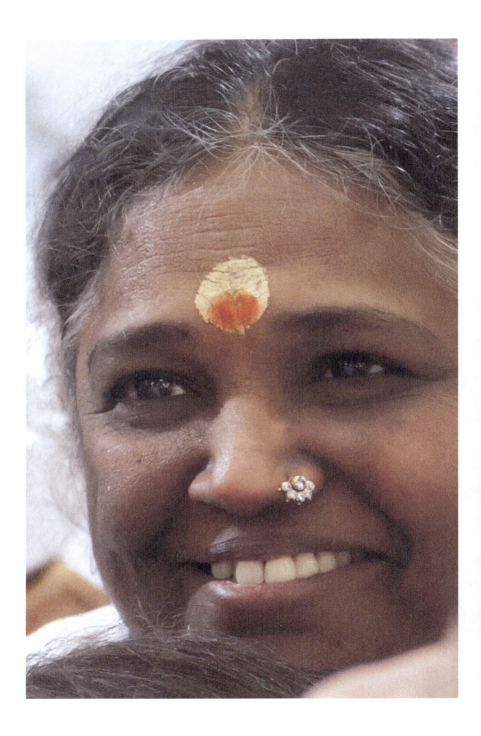

Chapter 14

Overflowing Compassion

*"The best way to find yourself is to
lose yourself in serving others."*

– Mahatma Gandhi

When we see how much Amma gives to the world, we should examine our own actions and ask, 'How much am I really giving back for all I have received?' We may have had many darshans over the years, but how much have we actually changed? Can we say that we have truly absorbed Amma's love and passed it on to others?

Have we deeply assimilated Amma's teachings? Can we honestly say that we have put in the effort to utilise what Amma has worked so hard to give us? Probably not…but Amma never judges anyone. She gives Her absolute maximum to us all the time, never asking for anything in return.

Amma knows we will receive back the exact karmic consequences we deserve depending on how we have lived our life, which is in essence why She is constantly urging us to move forward and higher. She is working on a long-term plan with each of us, and even if we are not worthy of anything She selflessly bestows, that never stops Her from continually giving us so much more than we can ever possibly understand.

Amma keeps on giving and giving and giving no matter where She is or to whom it is. She cannot help Herself. It is simply Her nature to overflow with compassion. We should think of how *our* nature manifests. We receive so much and still we demand more. How much do we actually pay back or share with others?

We cannot keep Amma's love all to ourselves. Love is not something that we can hoard away thinking, 'The love I get from Amma is for me alone.' It is a very lonely place when we simply dwell in a memory of love.

Only when you share your love with others will your heart's essence blossom and grow. Then love will become a living force that overflows and exudes an exquisite fragrance to the world.

One time after Amma finished giving darshan, She said to me, "Three times I started to lose consciousness during the darshan." People do not realise; everyone is so wrapped up in thinking about what they can *get* from Amma. They never think about how hard it is for Amma's body to go on like this day after day.

At the end of this particular public darshan, Amma went into the camper and we started driving to devotees' houses to perform pujas in their homes. It was two p.m. and Amma had just finished giving darshan all night and all day. She had started the program at seven the evening before and finished seventeen hours later. We were all thinking the same thing, 'How is it even possible that Amma can do this?'

Immediately after finishing darshan and entering the vehicle She was fresh and ready to go out again and give some more. Several devotees had invited Her to their homes, asking Her to perform pujas for them. She refused to rest at all before these house visits. I said to Her, "Amma, You didn't even use the bathroom!"

She replied, "Oh, it doesn't matter."

...And all of this was *still* not enough for Amma. She wanted to give more.

We cannot comprehend the exalted state in which a Mahatma like Amma dwells. She just keeps on giving, but no matter how much She gives She always remains over-flowingly full. In fact, Amma seems to glow even more brightly at the end of darshan than at the beginning. Even though Her sari may be stained with the makeup and tears of the people She has embraced and Her hair may be a little messy, She is absolutely incandescent as darshan draws to a close. Just one look at Amma's face shows how much joy She receives from the love She gives.

On the day of the seventeen-hour darshan, after the house visits, we got into the car, and someone enthusiastically passed a gift for Amma through the window. It was a pot of prasad they had made. There I was sitting with this big bowl of prasad on my lap, not knowing where to put it with all of the other bags that lay at my feet.

As I opened the lid, Amma saw what was inside: peanuts, boiled peanuts. They were very oily and mixed with coconut. It was a big bowl and there was a spoon inside. Amma wanted to share something with the people standing outside the car and took full advantage of the opportunity saying, "Oh, I can give prasad!"

It was not enough for Her to give darshan for seventeen hours, nor was it enough to go on several house visits afterwards. Amma would only be content after She handed out prasad to everyone as well.

I had the spoon ready, but instead of using it, She dug Her Hand right into the bowl and handed the peanuts out through the window. Peanuts soared in all directions – and these were not dry little peanuts.

They were greasy, coconut-oily peanuts, and the coconut was getting everywhere. As I looked around the car I thought, 'Oh my goodness. What are they going to think happened when we arrive and someone has to clean the car!'

The peanuts were flying and Amma was giving to everyone out of the car window as we were driving off. She just could not control Herself. Her only thought was to keep on giving.

As we started to drive onto the road, people began coming out of their houses and were running down the road following us. At that point, I was thinking, 'Enough, Amma. It's enough. You've given enough to these people. You do not need to give to every single person who is running along the road!' But Amma wanted to, so She kept on handing out more and more prasad as we were driving. Handfuls of peanuts were going out of the car window and everyone was so happy.

Amma was beaming with joy, and I was sitting there saying, "Amma, the peanuts are everywhere!" They were all over Amma, all over me, and all over the car. She must have given sixty handfuls of peanuts out of the window.

At long last we closed the windows and found ourselves sitting there, covered from head-to-toe in peanuts and flecks of coconut. Amma said, "Yes, they are very oily…" Then, She decided that we all had to have prasad as well! So She grabbed another handful and gave to Swamiji, the driver and me.

The peanuts were not only in the back now, but all over the front of the car as well. There we were, all happily sitting in this little grove of peanuts – they really were splashed everywhere.

Amma was blissfully happy to have given and given, until the last peanut was almost gone. After all of that giving, She glowed even more. In that moment, it was obvious how undeniably superhuman Amma's behaviour is. While we keep ourselves completely limited in all of our humanness, Amma has shot way beyond gravity's pull.

When we forget about our own needs, the universe with all of its cosmic power flows into us to refill us. No one has ever embodied this truth more than Amma.

When darshan programs are finished, all I want is to go to my room, close the door, have something to drink, and lie down to get some rest at last, but not Amma. She takes hours and hours to unwind. She reads devotees' letters, works on preparing Her next satsang (memorising it so that it can be translated into different languages), makes phone calls to give advice, and makes sure that everyone else (including the dogs) has eaten – all before She will take Her one meal of the day. That is Her life.

We should contemplate on Amma's example and think deeply. Service done with the correct attitude really does have the power to purify us. Amma guarantees this. Are we making the most of our precious life? We are so blessed to have the opportunity to do seva and serve others.

Are we making proper use of the gems that life has offered us? We owe such a debt of gratitude to this whole universe; someday we will have to pay it back. Why not start now?

There is a seventy-year-old devotee who works long hours doing seva in the bakery, but she is so happy to serve. She said that she has developed muscles now. She stirs the big vats in one direction, then in the other, hour after hour, and has become fitter and stronger than ever before as a result of all the hard work.

I heard Amma say one day, "I would rather bow down to a worldly person than to a spiritual seeker who is lazy." Someone who is out in the world working hard and honestly, with a good attitude, is really much more spiritual than a lazy person who wears sacred ash on their forehead to show how spiritual they are.

You do not even have to believe in God if you are working hard in the service of others. There are so many atheists who have service-minded jobs helping other people, serving the world with such a beautiful attitude. This dedication initiates a purification process in their lives, whether they know it or not.

No matter how many mantras we recite or how many hours we sit in lotus posture for meditation, the thoughts in the mind may still whirl about focused on, 'me, myself and I…what I want and need…' We have to develop a service-minded attitude in order to take us out of our orbit of selfishness.

Amma will not force us; the desire to change must come from within. She understands the real nature of people and the world and has no expectations from anyone or anything outside of Herself. This does not mean that She is devoid of feelings for us; on the contrary, Amma loves us more deeply than we can ever possibly imagine.

Chapter 15

Unshakable Love

"You know why it's hard to be happy? It's because we refuse to let go of the things that make us sad."

— *Lupytha Hermin*

Love and service are the highest forms of *sadhana* (spiritual practices) we can ever aspire towards. Yet they can only be achieved, in their fullest sense, through the practice of detachment.

We know that we should love people and make use of worldly objects. Instead, we tend to love material objects with all of our heart, clinging onto them, and make use of people for our own benefit, only to discard them when they are no longer useful.

It is Amma's refined sense of detachment that allows Her to love us so deeply and unconditionally. Detachment does not mean remaining aloof and disinterested. When we have authentic detachment, a complete fullness wells up within us. It arises because we understand the true nature of the people and

137

things that we encounter; we know they cannot give us lasting happiness.

Every day Amma shows us the perfect example of how to live in the world, channelling the correct emotions for every situation. She pours Her heart into every single interaction, meeting people one after the other, deeply sharing Her heart with everyone through their joy, pain and sorrow. But at the same time Amma is never attached or shaken by anything or anyone.

She accepts and forgives the fickle state of our mind. Amma feels only empathy for everyone who comes to Her, and yet, no one can pull Her down out of Her calm, centred existence.

Most of us get caught up in the habit of viewing things negatively at some time or another, but Amma never falls into the trap of getting caught up in any kind of negativity. Unlike us, She remains detached and simply allows emotions to pass through Her.

At times we all live in a fantasy world of our own creation. We shape visions of how we would like things to be, filling our fantasies with all of our hopes and dreams, but the eventual outcome of events is usually far from what we ever imagined.

Amma knows the ultimate truth: She understands that the people and things we cling to will never be able to fulfill our dreams (they will probably only contribute to our nightmares instead). If we can acquire even a little detachment it will bring us peace and contentment, and will save us from needless heartbreak in this ever-changing world.

A man came up to Amma for darshan and asked Her for a wife. His desire was fulfilled quite quickly, and he was married soon afterwards. A short while later he came back to Amma and said with a little embarrassment, "Amma, uh…I changed my mind. Could you please take her back?" Such is the nature of our vacillating minds. Only when we discover the inner relationship with our own Self, will we truly satisfy our needs and desires, finding fulfillment.

During our journey through life we will meet thousands of people and feel all sorts of emotions for them. But instead of developing a degree of inner detachment towards people, we constantly indulge in feelings of likes and dislikes and often let these emotions completely take us over. We remain a slave to our sensory perceptions.

A while back, at the end of the bhajan program while Amma was sitting on the stage during the arati, some babies crawled over to Her and Amma took them onto Her lap. After the arati, Amma went off to another room. She had a few minutes to spare while She waited for the sound crew to set up so that She could record more bhajans. In the few minutes Amma had to Herself, She asked me to bring the babies.

I went out and looked around, but I could not find any babies anywhere. There were other people looking at me with longing, but they were really far too big. The babies must have gone to bed early or something. So I had to go back and tell Amma that I could not find any babies.

Amma loves children. She will play with them and give them love. She will totally reflect their complete innocence back to them, but still She remains detached on the inside. One time I asked Amma how She could love the children so much. She said, "Yes, Amma adores children. She loves to hear their little cooing voices…"

We looked at each other and smiled. I finished Her sentence, joking, "…But after a few minutes, She is ready to give them back to their parents because they start crying!"

While living in the midst of temptations, we need to understand the real nature of worldly objects and the limitations of our worldly relations. Pure love does not lessen through detachment. True detachment brings us only stronger and deeper love. Without this understanding, suffering is inevitable.

Wherever we go in the world, we should understand the changing nature of it, not paying too much attention to the endless ripples of thoughts and emotions that course through us. Amma is always reminding us that we cannot get any permanent happiness from this ever-changing, impermanent world. Ultimately we are forced to go inside of ourselves if we want to find the source of genuine, lasting happiness.

Once there was a great Jewish sage who had two sons. One fateful afternoon, both of her sons were struck by a terrible illness and died almost immediately, before any help could be called.

The two boys died on a holy day and according to Jewish law, Jews are commanded to be happy and grateful on that day. Somehow she managed to push her grief aside, and with true strength, forced her mind to remain joyful, full of faith and love, throughout the entire day.

When her husband came home and asked where the children were, she did not want to upset him. She told him casually that they had gone out.

At sundown, when the holy day ended, she presented a dilemma to her husband: she told him that many years before a man had come to her and entrusted her to look after two very precious jewels.

He had recently come back to request the return of his property. What should she do?

Her husband responded that what was entrusted to her had never belonged to her and she must return them. She agreed and told him then that God had come to collect their two sons.

Hearing that his beloved sons had died, the husband wept. But his wise wife comforted him saying, "My dear husband, didn't you yourself say a moment ago that the owner has a right to reclaim his property? God has given, and God has taken away. Blessed be the name of God."

The sage gives us a powerful example of detachment in this story, but don't misunderstand the message. Amma is not saying that we should be happy when terrible things happen in our lives. She is simply teaching us to remember the ephemeral nature of this world: everything and everyone in creation eventually goes back to its source. Everything belongs to God alone.

Amma repeatedly reminds us that we come into this world with nothing and we leave again in exactly the same way, with nothing. There is no person, object or possession that truly belongs to us.

Only when this understanding has established itself in our heart will our attachments and negativities begin to fall away naturally and permanently. God alone accompanies us throughout the whole journey – and She is holding us close the entire way.

If we force detachment on ourselves too quickly, before the time is right, pushing ourselves into certain emotions or stances without the correct understanding – it is not going to get us to where we want to go. We will only end up suffering miserably instead. If we insist on trying to force our attachments to leave, without dissolving them with a mature mindset, they will probably all rush back accompanied by their noisy friends, jealousy and discontent.

Many times in Amritapuri, people come to stay 'forever' and want to dive headlong into the most intensive forms of sadhana and *tapas* (austerities). They long to become modern-day ascetics; they beg Amma to crush their ego. Then when things do not go exactly like their ego thinks it should, they are very fast to run off screaming and complaining about everything. How easy it is to forget that all is the Divine will.

When we deepen our understanding and genuinely know what we want in life, why we want it, and how to reach that goal, then all of the things inside of us that stand in the way will spontaneously fall away on their own when the time is correct.

The main, magic ingredient that will take us where we want to go is grace. It is so easy to earn grace from Amma, but the process of making ourselves fit recipients for that grace can be very difficult. It takes sincere effort, rooted in discrimination, to hold onto the grace that Amma constantly showers upon us.

People are often overwhelmed and deeply touched by Amma's presence, but do they even make the effort to come to the next program? It is sometimes too much effort to travel even short distances, although Amma travels all the way across the world to see us. So many people are unprepared to make any effort in their lives for the most important things, but will move mountains for mere trifles. We expect grace to come to us without effort, but this rarely happens.

I remember meeting a Chinese lady from Malaysia who was extremely moved and uplifted by Amma's darshan; her heart overflowed with emotion. As she was leaving to go back home, I spoke with her and suggested that she come to the next program as well. "After all, it's only three hours distance away," I pointed out.

"No," she replied, "that's too far."

We want to achieve our birthright, to drink from the fountain of wisdom that lies within, but we refuse to make even the most basic efforts. If we continue on in this way, the goal will remain so close and yet so far from our reach.

There is a magic formula to help us attain success: grace plus effort, combined with the correct understanding. This will lead us to success. When we put in our best effort while maintaining an innocent attitude in our heart, Amma's grace will spontaneously and naturally flow towards us.

Only when we have learned to serve selflessly, without attachment, without judgment and without expecting anything in return, will we be led towards true love.

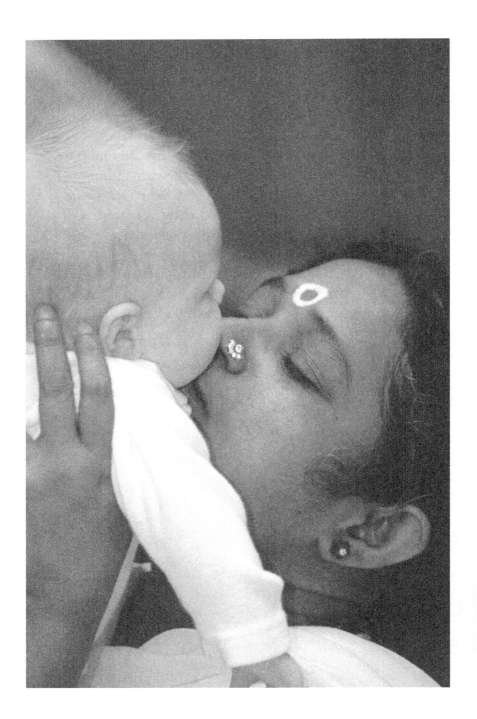

Chapter 16

The Faculty of Discrimination

*"It is better to walk alone than with a
crowd going in the wrong direction."*

– Diane Grant

We should strive to connect to others *without* our
feelings and emotions clouding us and taking us over.
When we are able to lift the veil of our emotional
influences it helps us to see more clearly the correct
way to move forward, and allows us to perform the
right action at the right time, with the proper attitude.

Performing good karma for dharmic reasons cuts
through our *vasanas* (latent tendencies); it is the
foundation on which *viveka-budhi* (discriminative
intellect) rests. It is the discriminative intellect that
pushes us to do good actions, but only when we do
good actions will the discriminative intellect flow; the
two go hand in hand.

When we use our discrimination we are asking ourselves, 'Is this really the truth behind my action? Is my action being coloured by my judgments, by my likes and dislikes, or am I doing the right thing? Am I heading in the right direction towards something good or further away from it?'

Discrimination means looking at things from the centre without being swayed to either side by our likes, dislikes or other emotional judgments. We should use the inherent quality of discrimination in all of our actions. But people so rarely do in today's action-packed world. As Voltaire, the French philosopher, once said, "Common sense is not so common at all; in fact, it is completely rare."

One day in the middle of the North Indian Tour I really needed some shoes, so I went to a shoe shop and someone talked me into buying an expensive new pair (something that I would never usually let myself have). They cost 1,200 rupees, which seemed to me like a fortune for a pair of shoes. The person I was with insisted that I needed them, saying, "They'll be good for you and good for your feet...these shoes will last for years." I really did not want to pay that much, but I finally agreed, ignoring the quiet voice of discrimination within.

The very next day we went with Amma to stay at a devotee's house, and I left my new shoes in the camper so they would not get lost. It started to rain, and the bramachari in charge of the program felt he would do us a great favour by taking our shoes out of the camper and leaving them by the front door. That way we could put them on when we left the house and avoid walking through the mud and puddles in our bare feet.

Unfortunately, when Amma left the house, She exited through the side door instead of the front door, and I quickly followed behind Her and rushed into the vehicle.

Later on, when we stopped by the side of the road for chai and dinner with everyone, I wondered aloud where my new shoes were. The shoe-moving bramachari turned up while I was in the middle of my search and admitted that he had taken my lovely, brand new shoes out of the vehicle and put them by the front door of the house we had just left. He had simply forgotten to tell me about his plan.

So there went my most expensive pair of shoes and I did not even get to keep them for twenty-four hours! At that moment, I realised that I should have listened to my own discrimination and gotten something less expensive, knowing that the shoes might not last so long on an Indian tour.

We should use the spiritual values we have developed in our life to help us make good decisions. Discrimination springs from the intellect, the heart, and the voice of experience. It is the intuition inside, that tiny spark of Divinity in us whispering, "This is the right thing to do." Discrimination is a quiet voice inside everyone always urging us on towards good. If you keep quiet, maybe you will hear it.

It is said that the faculty of discrimination is the only difference between animals and us. Other than that, our actions are the same. Both animals and humans take food and defecate; we both love our offspring and will defend them whatever the cost. There are not as many differences between people and animals as we tend to think.

Animals simply follow their natural instincts. But even so, they are not at all as selfish as we often can be. In fact, animals' natural instincts are often purer and much more developed than our own. We all know what dog spelled backwards is!

Take for example, the few stray dogs who wandered into the ashram a few years ago: these abandoned pups made their way right into Amma's heart and have been living in Her room ever since. To be honest, the dogs are more disciplined than most people. They go to archana every morning and to scriptural classes. In the evenings they faithfully attend the bhajans. Tumbhan, the male dog, always sits on the peetham next to Amma, while Bhakti, the female dog, occupies the humblest place of all, underneath the peetham below Amma. Bhakti knows the correct way for a spiritual seeker to behave. She always waits for Amma to be seated first before she delicately crawls under Amma's seat.

I remember a few years back when Amma went for Her birthday program across the river; Bhakti was there to see Amma off in the morning. And who was patiently waiting for Her at the very same place more than twenty-four hours later? Bhakti. It was Bhakti who humbly waited to receive Amma home again.

Although we are supposed to have discrimination, and it is said that animals do not, only people carry around the heavy burden of selfishness and ego.

The scriptures tell us that we evolve from plants to animals, from animals to human beings, and eventually, from human beings to God. One day we will all get absorbed into Divine consciousness and come to understand who we really are. But if we do not use our power of discrimination, we will never rise to that highest state.

Amma says that the teenage years are when all of our animalistic tendencies begin to bubble up inside. Current scientific experiments are proving this as well. Scientists are now teaching us that young teenagers do not have the power of discrimination because the frontal lobe of the brain, where reasoning power resides, is not completely developed at that age. This explains why children and teens tend to make decisions without thinking about the consequences of their actions.

A few years back during a retreat program in Seattle, one man was dutifully carrying out his seva serving the chai during a meal. A few small children came up to him and asked for chai. He felt they were too young to be drinking chai, so he told them they could not have any and refused to serve them. They were not happy about this at all. Placing their hands on their hips they demanded, *"We Want Chai! We Want Chai!"*

"No," he replied, "You can't have it!" One small child came around the table to where he was. The man bent down to speak to this little boy. But before he knew what hit him, the child reached up, grabbed his hairnet (all the food servers must wear hairnets) and pulled it right over his face.

As the man struggled to free himself from the hairnet, the other kids grabbed a few glasses of chai and they all ran off. The startled man realised he had been robbed by a gang of chai thieves, all less than eight years old!

In adults, the discriminative power should be stronger, as our brains are fully developed. But we must exercise this power and be aware that there are consequences for every action that we choose. Once we have grown older and more mature, and learnt from life's experiences, we should be able to use more discrimination. Using our discrimination does make it stronger.

One of Amma's teenage devotees told me that when she went away to University, she faced some unexpected, tough struggles. She had never drunk alcohol or taken drugs in her life; then all of a sudden she found that they surrounded her at every turn. Sometimes even her professors offered her drinks, and there were times when whole rooms full of students were high on drugs.

She felt very tempted to try these forbidden substances, but held herself back because she remembered Amma's teachings. Everyday when she chanted Amma's 108 names, she recited the mantra, "Salutations to Amma who strongly disapproves of qualities like stealing, injuring others and using intoxicants." Amma's names gave her strength, but her inner battle to avoid temptation became more and more challenging. Finally, she decided to speak to Amma about it.

Amma told her that it was her proper use of discrimination that held her back from making a dangerous mistake. Amma further said, "Drugs and alcohol are like fire. You know to keep your hand out of it because you are too smart to let the flames burn you."

Just keeping company with Amma infuses us with so many good qualities that we might not otherwise have; it is almost like a kind of spiritual osmosis. The company of a Saint always provides a conducive atmosphere for us to grow spiritually. By showing us Her own interactions with everyone in so many different situations, Amma teaches us how to be thoughtful and use our discrimination.

We need to listen to the voice of discrimination quietly whispering inside of us; it is always waiting to be called upon, but we all too often neglect it. Sadly, although we are endowed with discrimination, we so rarely use it. This is the main reason why we suffer so much.

We need to pull our discrimination into the forefront and make choices from a conscious level of awareness, remembering that there will always be consequences to every action we make. Our choices have the power to draw us closer to God, or push us further away.

Remove the obstacles that obstruct your path by using your discrimination in every situation. This power really does rest within us. Try to have the attitude of an innocent child who listens to his mother. We must try. Amma forgives any mistakes that we make. Have no fear; if you fall down due to your misjudgments, you only land in the lap of the Divine Mother – there is nowhere else to fall.

Once we learn the art of discrimination, we will always be smiling within – no matter what explosions and eruptions of chaos might be threatening us on the outside.

Chapter 17

Learning to Choose

"What day is it?" Asked Pooh.
"It's today." Squeaked Piglet.
"My favourite day." Said Pooh.

— A.A. Milne

It is impossibly difficult to free ourselves from the 'stickiness' of the mind; it traps us every time. The human mind is enormously complex, unrelenting, and unfortunately for us, we are stuck with it…and we really do get stuck.

Despite our most sincere hopes and wishes, the mind will never settle down and become our friend because it is programmed to search for pleasure (but instead it usually finds only misery). Until we reach the state of God-realisation, the mind will always wander from the truth and try to drag us along with it.

It is said that the goal of human life is to find true happiness, but our mind wants to search for it in all the wrong places. It is so easy to be fooled; after all, so much of who we think we are is the product of the ungovernable, wandering mind.

This is why spiritual traditions provide so many different methods to help us step back and become a witness to the unending stream of thoughts that flow through us. These techniques help us to still the mind and free us from the sticky thoughts and emotions that want to attach us to all the wrong things.

In truth, you are not your mind; you are not your body; you are not your emotions. You are the pure Self that is always silently watching, but maya stubbornly covers this Self with a thousand whirling thoughts.

It is this mindset full of attachments, which has caused us so much suffering. We are completely identified with our body and emotions; therefore, it is difficult for us to even imagine that our true nature is the ever-free *Atman* (Supreme Consciousness).

We say that we want to progress spiritually, but if we are simply fulfilling our duties without opening our heart, we will not be able to move forward. We know the correct thing to do in most situations, even if we do not always do it. But we should strive to follow what is right, even when we do not feel like it. This will help take us beyond our limitations.

We were on the plane one day, on a small flight going from Mauritius to Reunion Island; I was sitting next to Amma when all of a sudden She took my hand and started to gaze deeply into it.

She was just about to tell me what She saw; She was on the verge of unfolding the secrets of all my lifetimes, when someone walked up to me in the aisle, tapped me on the shoulder and whispered, "Can I ask Amma a question?"

My shoulders sagged a bit, and I hesitated for a moment. I mean, how often does one get the chance to have Amma read your past and future? But what else could I do?

I reluctantly put on a smile and replied, "Yes…" That moment with Amma was gone. We never did get back to it.

It can be hard at times, but try not to listen to the mind too much; it will always attempt to pull you away from doing what is right. The mind tricks us by justifying everything with its own twisted logic. It will tell us things like:

Chocolate comes from cocoa, which is a tree.

That makes it a plant. Therefore, chocolate is salad!

We will advance only by willingly going beyond the bare minimum that is required. If we really want to grow spiritually, it is essential to develop discrimination and learn to distinguish between the eternal and the non-eternal.

We must understand what choices will lead us to lasting happiness and bliss and which will bring us only temporary moments of joy (and ultimately suffering). Using our discrimination means choosing to move closer to God in every single decision that we make.

One boy who was visiting the Amritapuri ashram found out Amma was giving private room darshan to ashram residents and was not available to give darshan to visitors. He left the ashram and went off to Varkala beach for a week, lamenting that he would not get the chance to see Amma.

While he was away Amma called all of the Western visitors to Her room and allowed them to sit with Her there for more than an hour. Everyone was extremely happy, everyone except this boy. When he returned from his beach holiday, he was deeply disappointed to hear he had missed out. This is how it is: if we are not alert, and we veer from the path, we will definitely lose precious opportunities.

We have so many disappointments in life because we do not use our discrimination properly.

We are the cause of our own suffering. When we use our discrimination we realise that every situation presents itself for a good reason. Pain comes to us because of our own past actions, but this can be difficult to understand because karmic consequences can go forward through lifetimes before they manifest.

Everything that happens to us is because of actions that we have performed in the past. Their results always have to be experienced. Nothing that happens is accidental; cause and effect always comes into play.

The correct attitude is that of acceptance. It is the only intelligent way of living. Acceptance and discrimination are one and the same. Only if we have a pure, open heart will we be able to adjust and adapt to all of the various situations in life.

Instead of holding onto this understanding, more often than not we fight our circumstances and project blame, judgment and anger on everyone and everything around us. We do not use our faculty of discrimination in the right way; instead, we twist everything to suit our ego.

When we dwell in our suffering by holding onto our painful experiences, instead of letting them go, it is because we have not looked at things in the correct way. Western psychology often urges us to relive it all, examining our pain over and over again, but Hindu philosophy teaches us to simply release it.

We are not seeing the world from the right vantage point, with the right perception. If we did, nothing could hurt us. Discrimination helps us to understand the truth: all of life's circumstances are only teachings that are waiting to be revealed to us. If we used our discrimination properly, we would never feel negative towards the people and situations that befall us.

This does not mean that we accept all kinds of behaviour; there is a time to rise up and say NO! when something is incorrect, for example, in cases of domestic abuse or other such situations of violence. There is a time to stand up when something unrighteous is happening and strive to stop it. But even while standing up for what is right, we should hold a certain level of detachment and discrimination in our mind (since no one wants to be told that they are wrong).

I will never forget the impact of a news report that I read once about a man who fell unconscious on the train tracks. A security camera captured footage of another man who jumped down onto the tracks as well. It seemed as if he was going to help the fallen man and save his life. Shockingly, the camera recorded the second man rummaging through the victim's pockets, stealing his valuables and then running off. He left the helpless man lying on the tracks, where he was sure to be run over by a train.

This event is absolutely horrifying, but unfortunately, it accurately represents the sad state of the world today. Instead of trying to help each other to rise, we are pushing each other down and stepping on others in order to climb higher, robbing them in the process.

We are made in the image of God, but we constantly forget how special we are. Amma embodies the Divinity that is inherent inside each one of us. She personifies the knowledge that the Divine is everywhere and acts from this realisation, with all the wisdom of the universe flowing intuitively to Her in every situation.

Amma uses Her discrimination perfectly and goes beyond all negative tendencies. She sees God in everything, in every particle of creation. This is the highest state we can aim for – to see God's hands everywhere. When we have this vision, we will understand why everything happens in this universe. From this knowledge a deep compassion for the suffering of all beings spontaneously arises within.

Amma has genuinely touched the greatest height that human potential can reach…and we have not. Nobody usually does because we do not try hard enough. Amma encompasses what we really are supposed to be (and has even gone way beyond that). The rest of us limit ourselves to mediocrity.

To look at Amma is to understand why we have this human birth and how noble it can be. To truly see Amma is to realise that Divinity actually does abide inside each one of us, and is within our reach.

One day a young man asked Amma, "What is the quickest way to enlightenment?"

Amma answered him, "Pursuing enlightenment is like when you are hungry and tired in the middle of the forest, and a lion is chasing after you. You do not care at that moment about the hunger or tiredness. You have all the energy in the world to run away from that lion. This is the attitude that we need to reach the goal.

Imagine that you are about to be hung and someone offers you a million dollars. It will not matter to you at all because you are trying to escape from the hangman's noose. You will not care about any material possessions at that time; you just want to get away from death. Your attitude is the thing that matters the most."

While living in the world, we need to understand the true nature of worldly objects and the limitations of our worldly relations. Without this understanding, suffering will be inevitable. Amma is always reminding us that we cannot get any permanent happiness from the ever-changing phenomena of this impermanent world.

The discriminative faculty teaches us to turn inside and realise our own true nature, which completely transcends the ever-vacillating waves of the mind. Only when we understand who we are, can we understand who everyone else is as well. It is from this understanding that we finally learn what it means to become a complete human being. Ultimately, if we genuinely want to find the source of lasting happiness, we are forced to go inside.

Amma knows Her true Self, and because of this, She has found the greatest bliss that can ever be attained. She has gone beyond the wavering mind and has quelled the restless thoughts in the coolness of unalloyed discrimination. She is 100 percent surrendered and lives with 100 percent faith in the Divine.

Our mind, on the other hand, is stuck, churning with overflowing thoughts and constant doubts. These will be with us until we experience complete realization. Luckily we also have the gift of discrimination – this can save us, if we use it.

Chapter 18

From Awareness to Faith

"In reality, there is no new message to deliver about spirituality. 'Everything is God, there is nothing else but God.' This is the only message. This is the single message in the Upanishads, Vedas, Bhagavad Gita and Puranas. When we say that there are 108 Upanishads, we should understand that it is actually, 108 different ways of conveying the same message."

– Amma, Guru Purnima 2012

If we can learn to use the mind properly by channelling all of our energy – our thoughts, ideas and dreams – into positive directions through spiritual practices, then life will become much easier for us. No one is promising that life will suddenly be completely smooth, but it can become filled with incredibly joyful experiences.

There is a brahmachari living in the ashram who never travels anywhere and is very shy to speak with Amma directly. He talks to Amma's photo instead and tells Her all of his problems in that way. When he went for his private room darshan with Amma, he did not ask anything at all, but Amma of Her own accord answered his inner questions one by one, in the exact order that he had shared them with Her photo.

He was stunned. At the end She asked him, "How do I know all of these things?"

He replied, "Amma, because you are Devi."

"No," She gently responded. "It is because you spoke to me in the photo." Amma really does hear us, no matter where in the world we may be. She Herself is proof that the power of love reaches far beyond the veils of time and space.

Too often we get stuck in our perceived limitations, which stop us from reaching our highest potential. The mind is always full of doubts, but the warmth of true love melts all the doubts away and allows our heart to find peace.

When we arrived in Madurai during the South India tour of 2015, Amma went directly into the hall to serve everyone a meal. It was Pongal, the Tamil Nadu festival of the New Year, which is the most important holiday for Tamilian people. Amma fed all of the devotees and sang bhajans with everyone. As we were finishing our meal, She asked if anyone wanted to share a joke.

One woman took the microphone and was about to speak when Amma looked at her and started laughing and laughing. The woman was deeply moved and immediately began to cry.

Through her tears, she told a story: the day before, her husband asked her to prepare some *payasam* (sweet pudding) for Amma, saying that Amma might ask her for some. The lady did not listen to her husband; she was too busy with her seva, arranging the transportation so that devotees could come to the program the following day.

She thought to herself, 'Amma will not want me to cook Her payasam. So many of Her devotees are richer and more influential than I am. I am no one special, why would She bother to ask me?'

When Amma walked into the hall She immediately turned to this lady and asked, "Where is my payasam?" The woman continued crying as she related all of this to Amma, repeating again that she had thought she was so unimportant.

Amma looked at her with indescribable sweetness and replied, "Nobody is insignificant to Amma. Amma loves everybody – no matter who they are. It does not matter to Amma if someone is in an influential position or just a housewife. Everyone is special to Her." Amma said that the moment the woman thought about making Her the payasam, She had received it.

Endeavouring to connect with Amma's realm of thought is a much more beautiful thing to do than getting lost in the maya of our ever-changing mind. We have to fill our mind with conscious awareness, and live in the present moment, instead of clouding the mind with all of the things that we most definitely are not.

The mind is constantly thinking something, dwelling everywhere (except in the present moment) and making itself right at home in whatever emotion happens to be passing through – and none of these are befitting the precious jewels that we honestly are. We tell our self, 'Oh, I am like this...' Then find we are stuck in a slump for a long time, totally fooled by the phantom of our emotions.

Those little voices we hear in our mind all of the time have no substance. They change almost every second: 'I hate this person; I feel jealous of that person; I am such a loser...' The mind repeatedly feeds us crazy versions of reality – and we totally buy into them over and over again like defenseless children.

Mindful awareness is our greatest ally in our battle against the mind. It helps us to realise that we are not all of the different thoughts that flow through us.

Sometimes when we consciously battle against these thoughts they grow even stronger. Trying to consciously force our thoughts and desires to stop is not really possible and will often only result in anxiety or depression. We should try to tame the mind with acceptance and detachment, while maintaining the awareness of our true nature.

Amma is our Philosopher's stone. When we direct our thoughts towards Her, we find that our dark impulses are transformed into light. She offers Herself as a vehicle to metamorphose our negativities into blissful thoughts connected to Her.

When we think of Amma, our mind is channelled in a constructive direction, which cuts into the harmful tracks it usually runs in. She smoothes us out and redirects us toward the Divine. In this way, we are actively re-programming our mind in a positive direction towards joy.

One year at the Japan program, an older man stumbled after Amma as She was leaving the hall. Because of the way he was carrying himself, it seemed as if he was an alcoholic or had some sort of medical problem. He was abusively yelling at the Japanese people gathered around him, even though they were all being very kind and respectful towards him.

When he came near Amma, his tirade stopped altogether and he just melted into sweetness. On the second day of the program he arrived early in the morning for meditation and came into the hall smiling and laughing, transforming into a very gentle man. Amma is the embodiment of love itself; She soothes the savage beast in all of us.

It is difficult to keep the mind filled with good emotions such as compassion, empathy and love, but spiritual practices like mantra recitation, meditation, charity and selfless service will help to keep us occupied with good things we will enjoy. When we help others we will definitely benefit from it and will acquire more self-discipline in the process.

When we feel our heart open up and go out to another person, embrace a child or wipe away the tears of a person in need, we experience the truth of selfless love. Love is the source of who we genuinely are. This is how Amma lives Her life and how She wants us to be as well.

There is a touching story about one of Amma's very sincere devotees. He spends much of his time volunteering in the ashram kitchen, even though he is a very poor man himself.

When his daughter's marriage date was fixed, he was a very happy man; but as the day of the wedding approached, his happiness turned to apprehension. He did not have enough money to conduct the wedding ceremony.

The invitation cards were all printed out, but only a very small number of people were invited due to the lack of funds. He decided to go for Amma's darshan and give Her the very first invitation card, hoping he might also get relief from the stress and strain he was going through.

The man took his token, waited in the queue for hours and finally reached Amma's outstretched arms. Overwhelmed with joy and sorrow, he handed the invitation card to Amma; but there were so many people surrounding Her that he was pushed aside in the crowd and missed his darshan. It was impossible for him to get back into the line, because he had already surrendered his token. The man was thoroughly dejected because he did not get to tell his problems to Amma.

Worry plagued him. How could he possibly come up with the money to conduct the wedding? He went to the canteen and sat there shedding tears. A friend of the broken-hearted father saw how upset he was and went over to console him. As they were talking, a devotee from Singapore sat down and joined them.

After hearing the story, the man from Singapore took an envelope from his pocket and handed it to the father, saying, "Take this and don't worry." Then he got up and left.

The old man slowly opened the packet and found that it contained 50,000 rupees. He was aghast. He felt there was no way he could accept the gift and ran after the devotee who had given it to him. When he caught up with him, he thanked the man but said that he could not accept such a large sum of money. He insisted that Amma would take care of all his needs and tried to return the envelope.

The devotee calmly replied, "You should consider the money as a gift from Amma; I won't take it back. It is for your daughter's marriage expenses."

Amma is not limited to Her physical body. She works through all of us and is always with us, whether we remember and can feel this truth or not. How wonderful are Her ways of showering grace upon us, often at times and in places we would least expect. Her grace is enough to help us live peaceful and contented lives, even amidst all the problems that arise.

One girl asked me, "What is the biggest key to happiness?" "It is very simple," I replied, "Forget about yourself. Think of others." Once we weed out the negativities growing inside, liberation will be found.

We will find ultimate freedom and bliss only if we live our lives based on correct spiritual principles, but we need a polestar to guide us. Amma selflessly offers Herself to the world as our polestar. Through Her guidance, one day we will know and experience the truth beyond any doubt, that I am the Self – I am pure consciousness, I am bliss. In fact, this is the real nature of everything.

Book Catalog
By Author

Sri Mata Amritanandamayi Devi

108 Quotes On Faith
108 Quotes On Love
Compassion, The Only Way To Peace:
    Paris Speech
Cultivating Strength And Vitality
Living In Harmony
May Peace And Happiness Prevail:
    Barcelona Speech
May Your Hearts Blossom:
    Chicago Speech
Practice Spiritual Values And Save The
    World: Delhi Speech
The Awakening Of Universal Motherhood:
    Geneva Speech
The Eternal Truth
The Infinite Potential Of Women:
    Jaipur Speech
Understanding And Collaboration
    Between Religions
Unity Is Peace: Interfaith Speech

Swami Amritaswarupananda Puri

Ammachi: A Biography
Awaken Children, Volumes 1-9
From Amma's Heart
Mother Of Sweet Bliss
The Color Of Rainbow

Swami Jnanamritananda Puri

Eternal Wisdom, Volumes 1-2

Swami Paramatmananda Puri

Dust Of Her Feet
On The Road To Freedom Volumes 1-2
Talks, Volumes 1-6

Swami Purnamritananda Puri

Unforgettable Memories

Swami Ramakrishnananda Puri

Eye Of Wisdom
Racing Along The Razor's Edge
Secret Of Inner Peace
The Blessed Life
The Timeless Path
Ultimate Success

Swamini Krishnamrita Prana

Love Is The Answer
Sacred Journey
The Fragrance Of Pure Love
Torrential Love

M.A. Center Publications

1,000 Names Commentary
Archana Book (Large)
Archana Book (Small)
Being With Amma
Bhagavad Gita
Bhajanamritam, Volumes 1-6
Embracing The World
For My Children
Immortal Light
Lead Us To Purity
Lead Us To The Light
Man And Nature
My First Darshan
Puja: The Process Of Ritualistic
    Worship
Sri Lalitha Trishati Stotram

Amma's Websites

AMRITAPURI—Amma's Home Page
Teachings, Activities, Ashram Life, eServices, Yatra, Blogs and News
http://www.amritapuri.org

AMMA (Mata Amritanandamayi)
About Amma, Meeting Amma, Global Charities, Groups and Activities and Teachings
http://www.amma.org

EMBRACING THE WORLD®
Basic Needs, Emergencies, Environment, Research and News
http://www.embracingtheworld.org

AMRITA UNIVERSITY
About, Admissions, Campuses, Academics, Research, Global and News
http://www.amrita.edu

THE AMMA SHOP—Embracing the World® Books & Gifts Shop
Blog, Books, Complete Body, Home & Gifts, Jewelry, Music and Worship
http://www.theammashop.org

IAM—Integrated Amrita Meditation Technique®
Meditation Taught Free of Charge to the Public, Students, Prisoners and Military
http://www.amma.org/groups/north-america/projects/iam-meditation-classes

AMRITA PUJA
Types and Benefits of Pujas, Brahmasthanam Temple, Astrology Readings, Ordering Pujas
http://www.amritapuja.org

GREENFRIENDS
Growing Plants, Building Sustainable Environments, Education and Community Building
http://www.amma.org/groups/north-america/projects/green-friends

FACEBOOK
This is the Official Facebook Page to Connect with Amma
https://www.facebook.com/MataAmritanandamayi

DONATION PAGE
Please Help Support Amma's Charities Here:
http://www.amma.org/donations

CPSIA information can be obtained
at www.ICGtesting.com
Printed in the USA
FSOW03n2053271015
12659FS

9 781680 372830